Loving & Livin Free: Learn To Heal From Narcissistic Abuse

A Proven Path To Freeing Yourself From Future Toxic & Narcissistic Relationship Using Self-Awareness & Emotional Intelligence

Author: Dr. Herman Kynaston

© Copyright 2020 - All rights reserved.

The content contained within this book may not be reproduced, duplicated or transmitted without direct written permission from the author or the publisher.

Under no circumstances will any blame or legal responsibility be held against the publisher, or author, for any damages, reparation, or monetary loss because of the information contained within this book, either directly or indirectly.

Legal Notice:

This book is copyright protected. It is only for personal use. You cannot amend, distribute, sell, use, quote or paraphrase any part, or the content within this book, without the consent of the author or publisher.

Disclaimer Notice:

Please note the information contained within this document is for educational and entertainment purposes only. All effort has been executed to present accurate, up to date, reliable, complete information. No warranties of any kind are declared or implied. Readers acknowledge that the author is not engaging in the rendering of legal, financial, medical or professional advice. The content within this book has been derived from various sources. Please consult a licensed professional before attempting any techniques outlined in this book.

By reading this document, the reader agrees that under no circumstances is the author responsible for any losses, direct or indirect, that are incurred as a result of the use of information contained within this document, including, but not limited to, errors, omissions, or inaccuracies.

Free Gift

This book includes a bonus booklet. This giveaway may be for a limited time only. All information on how you can secure your gift right now can be found at the end of this book.

Table Of Contents

BOOK DESCRIPTION 3

INTRODUCTION 5

CHAPTER 1 PSYCHOPATH 101 7

Who Are Psychopaths? 7

The lack of empathy 8

Lacking the feeling of disgust 9

Low-intensity emotions 9

They're irresponsible 10

Lying and insincerity 10

A slightly 'off' way of speaking 10

Overly confident 11

Narrow attention 11

Egocentricity and selfishness 11

The lack of a sense of a bigger picture 11

How are Psychopaths Different from
Narcissists and Sociopaths? 12

Where Psychopathy Comes From 16

The Types of Psychopaths 17

Business psychopaths 18

The primary psychopath 18

Secondary psychopaths 19

High-functioning psychopaths 19

Impulsive psychopaths *20*

What's typical for psychopaths in work environments? *20*

How to Spot a Psychopath 21

They don't have fear *23*

They often switch jobs *24*

The Lack of Facial Expression and Empty Eyes *24*

They tend to speak in a monotonous voice *24*

Lack of attachment and profound emotions *25*

They disregard all rules *26*

They're shameless *26*

They will lie to your face *27*

They were a bully *27*

CHAPTER 2 SHADES OF A PSYCHOPATH 30

Do Psychopaths Know Love? 30

Why psychopaths want relationships *30*

How Psychopaths Use 'Love' to Manipulate? 32

Emotional Machiavellians *32*

Charm *33*

Flawed logic *33*

Insult and slander *34*

Emotional fog *34*

Evasiveness *35*

Deflecting guilt *35*

Lies *35*

Emotional deception *36*

Distorting the truth *37*

What to Expect from a Relationship with a Psychopath? 37

Stages of psychopathic seduction 38

The Dangers of Relationships with Psychopaths, Sociopaths, and Narcissists 42

The Worst-Case Scenario 44

How to Protect Yourself? 44

Be safe 45

Avoid them at all costs 45

Prioritize yourself 45

Be spiritual 45

CHAPTER 3 FEMALE PSYCHOPATHS 46

How to Spot a Female Psychopath? 46

Two-faced 46

A fierce competitor 47

Stalking and bullying 47

Warning Signs of Female Psychopaths 47

They make you feel guilty 47

Overly pleasing 48

What is the 'Love Bombing' stage? 48

Differences between Male and Female Psychopaths 50

1. Submissive 50

2. Passive-aggressive 50

3. Dramatic 50

4. Always a victim 51

Female Psychopaths and Relationships: Who They Target and How It Ends? 51

1. Control 52

2. Money loss 52

3. Drama and threats of suicide 52

CHAPTER 4 A PSYCHOPATH 'IN LOVE' 55

Psychopathic Romance: How They Operate...................... 55

1. They move fast...56

2. They're deceitful..56

3. They're controlling and possessive............................57

4. They're demanding 57

Psychopaths and Divorce... 58

How psychopaths act in divorce and in battle for custody...............58

How to survive a divorce from a psychopath 58

Unpredictable...63

Ambiguous 64

How to Stay Safe 64

1. Focus on your emotions..65

2. Be brave..65

3. Point out their flaws...65

4. Build up your mental power 65

5. Don't provoke them..66

6. Monitor their actions...66

7. Be diplomatic 66

8. Avoid meeting them 66

CHAPTER 5 CONSCIOUS DEFENSE:
HOW TO RESIST A PSYCHOPATH 68

How to Protect Yourself against Psychopathic Influence........................ 68

1. Look at the bigger picture..69

2. Avoid taking things personally and blaming yourself 70

3. Question everyone and everything 70

What Are the Psychopath's Weaknesses? 71

1. They dread loss and abandonment 71

2. They feel profoundly helpless and weak 71

3. They hide their weak spots 72

How to Be Immune to Psychopaths 72

1. Give only to those who give back 72

2. Prioritize your own well-being 73

3. Work to heal codependency 73

4. Prioritize your goals and financial growth 73

5. Define boundaries 74

6. Nurture healthy self-image and self-esteem 74

7. Rely on your support system 75

Learn How to Influence and Defeat Psychopaths 75

1. Map out your insecurities 75

2. Be unemotional 76

3. Boost your emotional intelligence 76

4. Criticize and point out their flaws 77

How to Divert Psychopath's Attention Away From Yourself.........78

Show them the most boring self 78

Make them think they won 79

Take away the reward 79

Learn that psychopaths have weaknesses 80

CHAPTER 6 TAKE PSYCHOPATH'S POWER AWAY WITH UNDERSTANDING 81

Give Them the Benefit of the Doubt: Are They All the Same? 81

Not all of them are violent 82

Not all of them are antisocial 82

Not all of them are toxic 82

What is the main point of understanding psychopaths? 82

Understand Their Emotional Disability 83

Acknowledge their inability to care 83

Remove the predator from your head space 83

Use their toxicity to learn about your value 84

Why psychopathy is a disability 84

How compassion for a psychopath helps you heal 85

Acknowledge Psychopath's Spiritual Purpose 86

CHAPTER 7 GET OVER A PSYCHOPATH AND FIND CLOSURE 88

Repair the Damage to Your Mind and Soul 88

1. Give yourself time 89

2. Heal codependency and own your identity 89

3. Build up self-esteem 89

Heal in the Aftermath by Finding Balance 91

How to balance your mind after abuse 91

Establish Strategic No-Contact 94

Create Lists and Compassionate Reminders 95

1. List your dreams and plans 95

2. Affirm your recovery 95

3. Move on 96

Use Self-Loving Mantras 96

CONCLUSION 99

DOWNLOAD YOUR FREE GIFT BELOW:..........................101

CHECK OUT OUR OTHER *AMAZING* TITLES:...............103

BIBLIOGRAPHY...129

Go from Stress to Success with These 15 Powerful Tips

You're in The Tunnel, Now Turn on The Light:

Here are The Best Ways to Transform Your Success

Do You Feel Stressed-Out, Overwhelmed and Harassed Every Day?

Then you're stuck in a negative thought spiral that is keeping you from achieving *real success!*

How many times have you thought, 'if only I could be more productive, then I'd get ahead?' No matter how hard you try, it eludes you. Most people experience intense self-doubt, worry and negative thinking at some point in their careers. These are your immediate obstacles to success.

This guide tackles these issues with easy, direct solutions to help you break the cycle and get back on track. These 15 powerful tips will take you from overwhelmed to overjoyed, in no time!

Dr. Herman Kynaston

This FREE Cheat Sheet contains:

- Essential tips on how to stop worrying and start living

- How to actually relieve anxiety and banish it for good

- Ways to get rid of negative thoughts, and how to stop them from recurring

- Tips to become the most productive, motivated version of yourself

- How to focus on career success and build positive cycles and habits

Scroll down and click the link below to Claim your Free Cheat Sheet!

I want you to know that you don't have to live this way. You don't have to feel like these negative cycles are getting the better of you. Your career is waiting to bloom – and flourish! Give yourself the opportunity to make the right choices, by learning how to authentically reach for lasting success.

Ditch the stress, embrace success.

Click Here!

Book Description

Emerge from a toxic relationship stronger, more powerful, and immune to psychological abuse in future relationships.

Does being with your partner leave you in an emotional fog?

Have you been conditioned to think you're not good enough?

A survey of hundreds of women found that a staggering 53% of them divorced their husbands on the grounds of emotional or psychological abuse.

Finding yourself locked into an abusive relationship is one of the hardest things you'll ever go through, but it's not something to feel ashamed of.

Whether you suspect you may be in a toxic relationship, or you've recently fought your way out of one, you need clear guidance to help you recognize the signs of an abusive relationship in order to heal from your trauma.

In *Loving & Living Psychopath Free*, you'll discover:

- The top red flags of emotional manipulation that may have been right under your nose all along

- Which of your personality traits your abuser exploited, and how you can stop it from ever happening again

- How to avoid making Rihanna's mistake: make sure you don't return to the **cycle of abuse**

Dr. Herman Kynaston

- The dangerous **lasting effects** your unhealthy relationship may cause unless you take action now

- How to **become a 'psychopath whisperer'**: understand the tactics your abuser used

- The secret to healing from guilt and shame

- The #1 surprising thing you can do to **take your abuser's power away**

And much more.

If your partner has left you feeling worthless, you might feel guilt, shame, or undeserving of love. This is the trap they've set for you in the hope that you'll be tied to them forever... but you're stronger than that.

Everything your partner made you feel about yourself is wrong. Show them they didn't beat you--take away their power *now*.

If you're ready to take back your control and disarm your abuser for good, then click "Add to Cart" right now.

Introduction

Are you fresh out of a toxic relationship or still gathering your strength to leave your abusive partner? If you feel like you are being manipulated to the point of questioning your sanity, this book is for you. In this book, you will learn the things you need to know about toxic and abusive individuals known as psychopaths, sociopaths, and narcissists.

In the beginning, your relationship was everything you dreamed about. Your partner was pleasant, funny, and kind. Soon after you've started dating, they professed their love for you and voiced their desire for a happy future together. Months, or even years later, you are still confused. Your life turned upside down, and the person you thought to be an angel who fell straight out of Heaven became your worst enemy. Soon after your relationship becomes serious, your partner started acting strange. Over time, they became cold, dismissive of your feelings, and cruel both in words and actions. No matter how hard you tried, nothing made them happy. You reached a stage of walking on eggshells to avoid upsetting them.

Somewhere down the line, you lost your sense of independence, and a future without your abusive partner or spouse became unimaginable. They were hard to live with, but you dreaded breaking things off and starting over. That is until they began making your life unbearable. They became more and more possessive and started controlling your activities, money, and social life. It could have happened that they became violent and abusive, and they broke your heart into pieces. Still, you wanted things to get back to the way they were. Regardless of everything you know about domestic violence and abuse, your story was unique. It was too good to end. You were under their spell until you eventually realized that the relationship had cost you too much. Perhaps, you fear it could cost you your life. Finally, you knew that there's something seriously wrong with your partner.

If this has been your experience, this book is for you. In this book, you will find out why your abuser acted the way they did. You may feel like the damage done to your body and mind is irreparable, but you'll learn the right strategies to recover and empower yourself.

This book will help you take your power back from the abuser, whether they're a psychopath, sociopath, or a narcissist. Moreover, you'll understand the tactics the person used to seduce you and gradually break your spirit. To understand why they'd want to do that, and why they've changed so drastically from the person you knew, you'll find thorough explanations of the mental disorders behind the abuse. Furthermore, you'll learn which personality traits of your own made you vulnerable to predators. You will also learn to use your innate kindness and care to support your own healing.

In this book, you will learn how to recover and overcome psychopathic abuse. You will discover that it is possible to rebuild yourself and reclaim your freedom, dignity, and power.

This book comes with a FREE Bonus chapter section as a gift. You can download them for free. The free content can be found at the bottom of this book.

Chapter 1
Psychopath 101

"He lives down in a ribcage in the dry leaves of a heart."

— *Thomas Harris, The Silence of the Lambs*

The recovery from systematic manipulation and abuse begins with the understanding of your abuser's mental disorder. In this chapter, you'll learn more about psychopathy as a mental disorder. By understanding how a psychopath's mind works, you'll be able to understand why they acted the way they did, and why you need to give up on the idea of changing them.

Who Are Psychopaths?

The terms 'psychopath' and 'sociopath' first appeared in the early 1800s. The psychiatrist who treated people with some mental health condition noticed that some of them, while appearing normal on the outside, had trades of so-called *moral depravity*, also known as *moral insanity*. These patients didn't have any sense of ethics or empathy for other people. However, they didn't share the usual traits of mental illness either. The term 'psychopath' was first applied in the 1900s. A couple of decades later, this term was changed to 'sociopath.' Psychiatrists used this term to highlight the damage that sociopaths caused to society.

The term psychopath was abandoned for a while and has only recently resurfaced. In science, the term is used to define a severe mental disorder. Aside from distinct personality traits, psychopathy links to many inherent genetic characteristics. Psychopathy is often used to describe a condition that has a more dangerous impact on society than that of common criminals. Unlike common criminals, people with this disorder had a skill of blending into society and covering up their crimes in the most devious ways. This ability made it a lot harder for authorities to uncover their wrongdoings, and the damage they caused extended beyond crime. They were able to influence others into committing crimes for their benefit, or even falsely confess the blame to protect a psychopath.

The term sociopath refers to people who are less dangerous and are seen as the product of the environment. While psychopathy is thought to be an inborn mental condition, sociopathy is society-induced. This means that people with sociopathy become such because of the way they were brought up, usually experiencing early trauma and neglect.

Psychopathy is a mental disorder that makes it impossible for a person to find love. Some of the most common traits of psychopathy include:

The lack of empathy

Psychopaths are known to be callous and lack empathy and regard for the world around them. This includes people, animals, and plants. They don't show any concern for the feelings of others. In most people, empathy is an emotion that's driven by their own sensitive nature. What separates the brain of a psychopath from that of regular people is a weaker connection in the parts of the brain that are in charge of emotions. As a result of this, psychopaths don't feel deep emotions. They are also not good at detecting them in facial expressions. If you ever wondered why your abusive partner or a family member appeared cold and emotionless, it was because they could've had an inborn inability to feel the same feelings that are common to most people.

Lacking the feeling of disgust

In a person's moral system, the emotion of disgust has an important role. We avoid doing certain things because we feel like they are disgusting and morally inappropriate. However, psychopaths don't have the same threshold for this. They have a lower threshold for feeling disgusted, which often results in morally undesirable actions. This explains why your partner didn't seem to have much understanding of the things that made you upset, whether in general or in the relationship.

Low-intensity emotions

Psychopaths don't experience emotions the same way most people do. They have a general lack of emotions, and those they do have are shallower than in most people. This particularly goes for embarrassment, guilt, and shame.

Psychopaths also have weaker affective reactions. That means that they have weaker expressions of feelings, both inner and outer. However, what makes psychopaths particularly dangerous is the fact that they feel and show little guilt. Most people avoid doing things that harm others because of their sense of guilt. It is not like that for psychopaths. Most normal people have a physiological response when they anticipate that something bad or painful will happen either to them or to others. Psychopaths don't have this kind of response.

They're irresponsible

It only makes sense for a category of people who are incapable of guilt and remorse to act irresponsibly. Psychopaths tend to blame others for their failures and rarely ever accept blame. Even when they are faced with evidence of wrongdoing, shame and remorse are non-existent to them. As such, they can't change their future behavior unless the risk of the outcome threatens them.

Lying and insincerity

Many psychopaths and sociopaths have superficial charm, which is an insincere form of behavior. Psychopaths and sociopaths act in inauthentic ways that range from pure insincerity to pathological lying. Psychopaths and sociopaths bend the truth so that it fits their interests and agenda.

A slightly 'off' way of speaking

Sociopaths and psychopaths have a different way of using words than ordinary people. They react differently to terms that depict emotions. For example, if you were talking about a sad event to an average person, they would alter their way of speaking and their body language according to the context of the story. It would affect their feelings. However, a sociopath or a psychopath doesn't do that. Since your story doesn't touch them emotionally, they rarely ever, if at all, react with facial expressions and body language.

What's particularly interesting about psychopaths and sociopaths is that they have a weaker understanding of abstract words and metaphors. Because metaphors require an understanding of the emotional background of a figure that is being described, they don't understand them.

Overly confident

Usually, psychopaths and sociopaths have a high sense of self-worth. This can go to can grow to delusional measures. Psychopaths and sociopaths believe themselves to be whatever they want. They don't require any external manifestation of skills or achievements to approve or validate their self-image. For this reason, they can have a delusional, grandiose sense of self that causes them to react to the smallest insults of their ego.

Narrow attention

Most people can change their responses to signals from the environment, depending on the relevance of information. However, psychopaths don't have this ability. This explains their impulsive nature, which is another criteria for this mental disorder. Psychopaths have problems with passive avoidance and processing feelings, which also results in their impulsive nature. However, their conscious attention is most often under control. Psychopaths aren't easily distracted and tend to have a better focus. This is the reason why high-functioning psychopaths and sociopaths can be successful in school and at work.

Egocentricity and selfishness

Most psychopaths and sociopaths are selfish and egocentric. They are mainly focused on themselves and their own benefit because they're emotionally detached from other people.

The lack of a sense of a bigger picture

Psychopaths rarely ever follow any life plans, and cannot plan for the future. They have a weaker ability to set long-term goals, and they rely on temporary gratification. A violent nature and a low tolerance to frustration explain why they will easily become violent. This happens because psychopaths have a lower threshold for expression of aggression. This causes them to be more irritable and aggressive.

How are Psychopaths Different from Narcissists and Sociopaths?

You might be familiar with psychopaths, as they're often present in movies and TV shows. In 2013, the TV series 'The Fall' presented the character of Paul Spector, a character that can serve as a good example of a psychopath. Paul Spector is an example of a high-functioning psychopath. While maintaining an image of a successful grief counselor, Paul Spector has a compulsion for strangling women. Outside the tendency to kill, Spector helps people heal from loss, and he's a devoted father who has endless patience for his children.

The more you learn about the character, the more you realize that his mental structure was created normally, but suffered irreparable damage. In the days of early childhood, his mother committed suicide, and the young boy was first to discover the body. His mother hanged himself, which was a scene he'd later recreate with his victims. After becoming an orphan, Spector was placed in a boarding school, where he suffered molestation by his mentor. Because of this experience, he became endlessly protective of children, which can be seen as his only positive trait. This is an example of the severe damage trauma can cause to a human mind.

Currently, researchers use a list of criteria to determine whether or not the person is a psychopath and to which degree. In 1941, the first list of criteria for diagnosing psychopathy was developed. It contained the first known detailed description of psychopathy. Any person who fell within the criteria was now known to be a sociopath or a psychopath. There are numerous lists that are being used in modern science to identify these mental disorders. Some of the most frequently used lists include PCL-R or the *Psychopathy Checklist-Revised*. There is also the PPI, created in 1996 by Andrews and Lilienfeld.

Most psychologists and psychiatrists use a particular book to diagnose and categorize either psychopathy or sociopathy, called *The Diagnostic and Statistical Manual of Mental Disorders*. It contains a category for a mental disorder called *The Antisocial Personality Disorder*, or APD. The World Health Organization uses a similar category called *The Social Personality Disorder*.

The terms psychopath and sociopath are commonly used to describe similar personality structures. While they're there are some similarities to the terms, there are also significant differences between psychopaths and sociopaths. What's common for both of these terms is that they describe a person who:

- is violent and criminal in their behavior

- lacks empathy for others

- is incapable of feeling shame and guilt

In psychiatry, both terms are used to describe a personality disorder known as 'Antisocial Personality Disorder,' which has a couple of distinct features. Both conditions share a couple of traits, like:

- disregard for the benefit of others that manifests in criminal behaviors like legal violations, deceitfulness to gain pleasure, and lying

- manipulating others for their own benefit

- the inability to plan and acting on impulse

- being irritable and aggressive, which often results in assaults on other people

- being reckless

- having a general disregard for their own safety, or the safety of others

- the inability to cater to adult responsibilities, like keeping a full-time job or taking care of their family and children

- a lack of guilt and remorse

These traits commonly result in serious harm to other people. There's a highlighted lack of empathy in both psychopaths and sociopaths. What both have in common is the disregard for others, interests, feelings, and rights.

They have a high sense of self-appraisal, which manifests in cockiness and extreme arrogance. While all of these are severe symptoms that manifest from early childhood, psychologists are reluctant to diagnose psychopathy in children. This is because children grow and evolve quickly, and no one can predict the direction to which they will develop. Even if a child can manifest ill-adapted and aggressive behavior, with the right influence, they can improve and grow up to become a well-adapted person.

Aside from these traits, psychopaths differ from sociopaths in their inability to attach to others emotionally. They usually have shallow and fake relationships that only exist to the degree to which it benefits them. They are prone to manipulation that benefits them and to act in authentic ways and charmingly to manipulate others. Sociopaths can have significant relationships, but they're also based on their own benefit and without genuine devotion.

Some psychopaths are also known as high-functioning psychopaths. They can keep the appearance of a completely normal person. Decades can pass before anyone notices anything strange about them, or they reveal their criminal acts. They only show their real face to people who are close to them.

On the other hand, sociopaths are capable of having close attachments to individuals and groups. They have great difficulties in forming relationships. Sociopaths usually have a hard time maintaining regular jobs or family life because they are impulsive and erratic. They are prone to anger, outbursts, and criminal activities, and have low adaptability to social norms.

Biological factors and the influence of the environment play a significant role in both mental disorders. Whether or not a psychopath or sociopath will be a criminal depends on the way they were brought up. Most of them will never function like an average person. They will never have stable emotional relationships. But, they can learn to live in a way that is not harmful to others. While psychopathy is considered to be an inherited condition that relates to the underdeveloped brain parts that are in charge of emotional regulation and the control of impulses, sociopathy mainly comes from a history of severe trauma and physical and emotional abuse.

You can say that psychopaths are a result of an extremely traumatic childhood, while psychopaths are born like that. Both of these disorders share some features with narcissistic personality disorder. This disorder, also known as the NPD, is typical for persons we call narcissists. Narcissists also lack empathy and have unrealistically high opinions of themselves. They also have shallow relationships and are prone to manipulating others. However, narcissists are rarely deceitful, aggressive, or impulsive. They usually don't have any tendency to criminal behavior. What makes them toxic is that their entire life revolves around their need for attention, admiration, and praise. Reduced abilities to care for others can hurt people around them and cause a great deal of emotional and financial damage.

Where Psychopathy Comes From

Psychopathy is thought to be mainly an inherited mental condition. While psychopaths express an extreme lack of empathy for others and can be highly manipulative, diagnosing the disorder is tricky. Unless there's material proof or a history of violent or criminal behavior, it's not easy to tell that a person is a psychopath. More so, because psychopaths tend to be so manipulative and deceitful as to manipulate even their psychiatrists.

It takes long observation and testing to get to know a psychopath. Under the surface of a seemingly charming person, they can have a total absence of conscience. While there doesn't have to be criminal behavior, there is always a potential for it.

The reason why psychopaths are so tricky to diagnose and treat is that they are disingenuous in words and behaviors but skillful enough to understand and give the desired response to a situation or a question.

Psychopaths don't react well to treatment. Both psychopathy and sociopathy are largely influenced by the person's upbringing. If these people were raised in abuse or neglect, they would be more prone to becoming criminals.

In psychopathy, genetics and brain anatomy play a significant role. Psychopaths have underdeveloped parts of the brain that regulate feelings. As such, they have problems experiencing love, kindness, care, attachment to others, and care for their wellbeing. On the other hand, they are unburdened with guilt or a guilty conscience, considering their minds revolve around them and their own benefit. Other people are merely tools for psychopaths to satisfy their needs.

The Types of Psychopaths

Psychiatry mainly distinguishes primary and secondary psychopaths, while criminology and literature also recognize other types. Primary psychopathy is thought to be mainly genetic, with an added impact of an unstable upbringing. While primary psychopaths have distinct, inborn traits in their brain structure, a traumatic past tends to worsen their condition. Opposite to that, a childhood without trauma and neglect creates better-adjusted psychopaths. It reduces the severity of their symptoms, giving them a sense of sadness when causing harm, or a sense of gratification for doing good.

The secondary psychopathy is mainly caused by the environment. A person can be born healthy, but suffer from underdeveloped emotions, moral system, and emotional regulation because of a traumatic childhood.

There are a couple of common types of psychopaths that vary in how they act, how well they regulate emotions, and how well they function in society. Knowing these traits might help you identify the psychopath. However, keep in mind that even well-educated psychiatrists take a long time to diagnose the disorder. Don't rush to call your ex-partner a psychopath unless they have an official diagnosis.

While psychopaths have almost no feelings under the surface, on the surface, they are quite capable of portraying genuine, kind, pleasant, and caring people. They also possess a vast amount of knowledge of what they should say or do to create the desired image of themselves. With that in mind, these are the following common types of psychopaths:

Business psychopaths

Research has shown that people in high positions in the corporate world tend to display more psychopathic features than others. They may push their subordinates over the edge and cause them to burn out. They use numerous strategies to advance at work, most of them unethical. Roughly estimated, some 1% of the population has psychopathic traits, and 4% of these people are thought to be business leaders. The highest amount of psychopathic traits is found in chief executives. When you work under them, they can cause a lot of stress and anguish.

The primary psychopath

A primary psychopath is a non-emotional person who acts in cruel and manipulative ways. While they don't have much fear or anxiety, they usually avoid risks. They also have absolutely no guilt or remorse. They are prone to acting in antisocial ways and are often associated with a narcissistic personality disorder. You will recognize them by the lack of sensitivity to others. These people will appear to show emotion only if it benefits them. Primary psychopaths tend to be perceived as smart, confident, and intelligent. They have a way of using their manipulation in ways that are socially acceptable but have harmful consequences in the long run.

Secondary psychopaths

Secondary psychopaths are mentally and emotionally unstable. They don't regulate emotions well and associate more with criminal behavior. They act on impulse and can appear emotional on the surface. They express feelings mostly in response to anger, sadness, grief, frustration, and provocation. They are prone to being self-destructive and aggressive. They make risky decisions and are disorganized in their appearance.

Secondary psychopaths usually have a small sense of remorse and some degree of empathy. They typically cloak these feelings in aggression and hostility because they are emotionally disturbed. Feelings are a weakness in their belief system, and they'll do everything in their power to defend from even a hint of guilt.

These psychopaths crave excitement and are easily bored. They usually strive to engage in dangerous and exciting activities as a way to find adventure. This type of psychopath quickly falls into a rage and is known to be aggressive and violent. You would call this type of man a 'hothead.' They are mainly males who enjoy dominance.

High-functioning psychopaths

These psychopaths use charm to advance and manipulate other people. They are also pathological liars. They are convincing because they lack any regard for the truth. They will use any false words or arguments, even made-up, to achieve what they want. Their charm helps them disguise their antisocial tendencies, which is the reason why they get away with crimes.

Impulsive psychopaths

These psychopaths are incredibly egocentric and prone to bending the rules to lie and manipulate. They do all this for personal gain. They rarely ever commit to long-term goals. Instead, they will do whatever it takes to gain the most advantage in the shortest amount of time. They are narcissistic. To them, the world is hostile. The world is 'the bad guy,' and they are the only 'good guy.' They see themselves as victims of the wicked world and unfavorable circumstances. They rationalize their behaviors using flawed logic and can be manipulative, deceitful, and aggressive. They'll resort to the most devious crimes while blaming others for the problems that they have caused to themselves. There is a strong association between this type of psychopathy and borderline personality disorder.

What's typical for psychopaths in work environments?

Psychopaths usually do well with other psychopaths, narcissists, and sociopaths. They'll quickly form a clique of the like-minded. This is because they have a lower response to stress. They also use many bullying tactics, like manipulating others into bonding. They build people up so that they can knock them down when convenient.

Using the information obtained from their pawns, they will establish control effortlessly. Then, they will abandon the victims who no longer serve them. Placing the blame on others and taking credit for others' successes, creating conflicts among their co-workers, and maintaining them to profit are only some traits of psychopaths.

The research has found that the greatest harm of having a psychopath at work is that they can create a toxic work environment. Whether in the area of career or personal life, they can be successful and cunning. Because they're unburdened by stress or morals, they easily focus solely on the numbers, doing the right things for their company. All this is for their own benefit, and if needed, they will create stress and conflict in the workplace to come out as a winner.

There are a couple of ways for you to cope with a psychopath at work. Some of them are:

- Understanding that their behavior can't change and it is a result of their insecurity

- Building a support team

- Knowing your rights

- Collecting material evidence and put everything in writing

- Establishing your own reputation and work relationships

- Controlling your emotions and avoiding showing fear

- Using online communication wherever you can, so it can be recorded and used if necessary

How to Spot a Psychopath

You are probably familiar with many psychopaths presented in the media. Characters like *Hannibal Lecter* or *Dexter Morgan*, portray highly intelligent, yet highly aggressive people who have an extremely low moral standards. Unlike psychopaths in the media, the behavior of real-life criminal psychopaths paints a different picture. When interviewing the criminal psychopaths, many news reporters are astonished by their ability to portray sensitive, well mannered, charming people. This exterior mask couldn't be further from what the evidence of their actions shows. Under the disguise of a likable person lies an extremely dangerous individual who might be sadistic and lacks any character features one might call human.

You might be dealing with psychopaths every day without knowing it. This is because they show their aggressive traits only when endangered. Part of the psychopath's charm is in the fact that they use peoples' apparent weaknesses to manipulate.

One of the ways to spot a psychopath is to identify passive-aggressiveness. They are delightful in their manners but phrase their words to subtly criticize and trigger insecurities. They exploit people's weaknesses. In their minds, your weakness is in your empathy, goodness, and everything you appreciate about yourself. They exploit vulnerabilities, mainly a person's need for security and love. They have the talent to notice your soft spots, which to them is having a big heart, a loving nature, generosity, and kindness.

Psychopaths also tend to act compassionately when talking in order to gain information they can use against you later on. An incredible charm is the main trait of a high-functioning psychopath. One of the crucial details that give out a psychopath is that they are flattering beyond reasonable measure. They praise and flatter without a genuine reason. A psychopath who is aiming to manipulate you will overly compliment you. They will say things you want to hear, regardless of reasoning and accuracy.

Psychopaths are good at understanding your deepest needs. A way for you to detect that someone is disingenuous is to question whether or not they are flattering you without reason. If a person acts overly serving and generous, they might not be genuine. Do they genuinely have a reason to tell you the things they tell you? Whether it's flattery or compliments, you can sense that the person is exaggerating.

In a relationship, a psychopath will start by treating you like the most important person in their life. They will tell you everything you want to hear to appeal to your insecurities. However, behind this is an intention to use you and to dominate you. They will also alter their behaviors to fit your taste.

You might notice traces of this in their behavior even if the reaction can't be described as socially undesirable or harmful. In everyday conversations, the psychopath will not be able to relate to any story of compassion. They will turn any discussion to facts, politics, or social justice, instead of talking about the emotional aspects of the conversation. They will laugh at your jokes because they understand that you want them to, but they won't laugh spontaneously. They won't notice something kind and funny unless it's pointed out to them. They are emotionally unresponsive. This means that if you display emotion to them non-verbally, they most likely won't respond.

They don't have fear

A psychopath won't be frightened by the things that usually scare people. They may disguise that as heroism. But if you encounter someone who appears to be unreasonably fearless, you can step back and question whether or not this behavior is normal.

They often switch jobs

A psychopath most likely won't tell you a story of a long-term, fulfilling career. Instead, you might hear a story that they are yet to find themselves in a specific profession, or that they are doing a temporary job until they find something better. They are inconsistent with work. They don't stay in the same job for a long time, because they can't hide their traits. Sooner or later, their features turn against them. When they feel like they can't be themselves at work, can't manipulate, or eventually get caught in a wrongful act, they will quit. On the other hand, they're prone to mischief that often gets them fired.

The Lack of Facial Expression and Empty Eyes

If you suspect that there's something 'off' about the person, look in their eyes and see if their look aligns with their words. Psychopaths somewhat lack facial expression, and particularly what you'd call a glow in their eyes. If you encounter a person who looks charming, but their eyes appear somewhat flat and empty, this can be a red flag. It is a different feeling than merely looking at a person who is a melancholic, tired, or sad. If you look into the psychopath's eyes, you will notice they look entirely lifeless. This is a stark contrast to their appearance, body language, and words.

They tend to speak in a monotonous voice

Psychopaths rarely raise their voices or express emotions through their voices. Most of us speak at a different pace when we are happy, sad, or angry, but not psychopaths. They talk calmly and flat on most occasions.

Lack of attachment and profound emotions

You might be wondering how a person can be so charming while the signs that there's something wrong with them are so visible. The answer to this is that they put on a show for you. They observe you and notice your insecurities. They notice what you want to hear and create the type of person you want to see. Then, they use their knowledge to put on a mask and disguise their detachment. But, the things that they can't fake are their look and their voice.

Given that psychopaths lack empathy, there could also be subtle clues revealing their detachment. You can check for them if you want to avoid a relationship with a psychopath in the future. Lacking empathy comes from a lack of understanding of emotions. Most people you talk to are emotional. Everything from their voice to body language is expressive of emotion and attuned to their mood and the tone of the conversation.

When talking to a psychopath, you'll find that they avoid using emotional phrases such as: "I understand;" "I like this;" "This hurts me;" "This hurts my feelings;" "This feels awful," and other phrases. Instead, they will talk in a more intellectualized way. They won't say that something makes them happy because nothing makes them happy. They may say, 'This pleases me" or, "This looks nice," instead. Looking into one's own expressions of emotion is a way to tell if a person is emotionally available. It is an excellent way to know if they have a genuine emotional response.

Psychopaths also are arrogant and entitled. They may not display this emotion in regards to you, because their goal is to win you over. However, they might act arrogant or insensitive to other people. If you are on a date, pay attention to how they treat other people around them:

- Are they acting friendly to you, only to be insensitive to a person who is serving you?

- Do they acknowledge and appreciate others' kindness?

- Are they prone to pointing out everything a person does wrong? Are they overly critical?

They disregard all rules

Psychopaths abide by the laws of society only to the degree to which it benefits them. They don't care about general morals. They don't think that rules apply to them, and you may discover this in subtle behaviors. For example, they might do something inconsiderate simply because no one is watching. If you're sitting at a restaurant, and smoking is forbidden, they might want to light a cigarette as soon as no one's watching. Pay attention to whether or not the person you are dating truly cares about their environment.

- Do they consider others, or find any limitation to be a nuisance?

- Do they make efforts to make people around them feel good, or they just do it for you?

They're shameless

Psychopaths lack guilt and remorse, and as such, won't feel awkward in any situation. You can easily confuse this for confidence. Genuinely confident people feel awkward in uncomfortable situations, but they're able to brush it off and laugh at the experience. If something embarrassing happens while you're around the psychopath, they won't acknowledge being wrong. They will act as if another person is to blame for what they have done.

- For example, let's say that your date accidentally spills a drink. Are they going to be funny about it or say that the restaurant has horrible glasses and the tables are too small?

They will lie to your face

A psychopath's goal is to portray an imaginary person and tell a fictional story. Accordingly, they will lie with no regard to the truth. They will casually tell a lie, but it can often be careless. They won't think about whether or not they can be caught in a lie. When talking to a person, pay attention to whether or not they have lied to you about irrelevant things. Have they lied about things that don't require lying about (e.g., what they did the other day, or what they had for lunch)?

They were a bully

The history of violence in early childhood and throughout puberty is typical for psychopaths. If you know someone who is a psychopath, it is likely that they were in trouble with the law, or had a problem at school for bullying, aggression, cheating, or theft. However, that doesn't mean that every child who is aggressive animals is going to turn out to be a psychopath. These behaviors can arise from many different reasons, like expressing rage dysfunctionally.

If children aren't taught how to properly show anger, it's only logical that they will express it improperly. However, if you realize that the person you're talking to, whether it's a coworker or a date, used to be aggressive, and that is a stark contrast to their behavior now, it should be a warning sign. If you caught them lying about their history, It could be a definite sign that they are at least unstable and unreliable.

Labeling someone a psychopath shouldn't be done loosely because even a therapist takes a lot of time and effort to make such a diagnosis. What you should do is to discover whether or not the person you are dealing with is genuine and honest, and if they have ulterior motives.

- If you are moving further into a relationship and you want to secure that this person is not a psychopath, look at whether or not they aim to be independent.

- Psychopaths are usually parasitic. They will put on a show of a provider for a short time, and then they will start making excuses for doing less housework and not bringing in money. Make sure to pay attention to whether the person is truly ambitious and whether they are capable of grasping long-term goals.

- In conversations, see if a person acknowledges the necessity of long-term hard work to achieve something, or if they are a so-called 'free spirit.'

- Another way to discover a psychopath is to look into your own thought process and see whether or not you feel like you're being manipulated. A genuine person who has your best interests at heart will give you space to be yourself. They will aim to get to know you and understand a bit more about how you think and feel.

- A psychopath always makes subtle efforts to lower your self-esteem by making ambiguous comments. If you meet a person who is flirting with you, they might tell you you're fun, pretty, attractive, or smart. Gradually, often after only a couple of dates, a psychopath will try to make you feel like you are only pretty and intelligent to them, not to the rest of the world. They will try to hint that other people around you aren't appreciating you enough, as much as they do.

- A psychopath will try to go beyond your comfort zone and talk you into doing things you are not comfortable with. For example, if you go out for a drink, and you only want to have a single glass of wine, they will keep talking you into having more drinks. The purpose of this is to establish control over your thought process.

- A psychopath wants to influence you. If you notice that you can't say a single thing without feeling like you're being influenced, it is a sign that you might be talking to a manipulative person.

Chapter 2
Shades of a Psychopath

"In situations of captivity the perpetrator becomes the most powerful person in the life of the victim, and the psychology of the victim is shaped by the actions and beliefs of the perpetrator."

— Judith Lewis Herman, Trauma and Recovery: The Aftermath of Violence - From Domestic Abuse to Political Terror

Do Psychopaths Know Love?

You are probably curious about whether or not psychopaths can feel love and other emotions. This largely depends on the individual and the severity of their mental disorder. While psychopaths can't feel love and have relationships for the sake of happiness, they do it for different reasons.

Why psychopaths want relationships

In general, psychopaths lack emotion or experience it only to a slight degree. Still, some psychopaths do show a normal degree or even hypersensitivity to some feelings. It makes the answer to the question of whether or not psychopaths can love complicated.

They need attachment

The first thing to address is the shallow nature of psychopath's emotion. Psychopaths have a different degree of sensitivity to different feelings. They are shallow when it comes to guilt, fear, and empathy. Still, they can experience happiness, but only a minimal amount. This is not the same intensity of the emotion as the ordinary person's. However, sensations like rage and anger are something that psychopaths can feel intensely.

Whether or not psychopaths love and how much are they capable of love depends on the degree of psychopathy. A psychopath's ability to love depends on the level of psychopathy and some degree of attachment is possible. Still, they are not likely to create secure connections. However, they will want to receive and take love, although they are unable to give it back. Despite this, psychopaths have relationships and marriages as a way of keeping up appearances.

They need company

Most psychopaths are aware that there is something that makes them different from the rest of the world and that they are emotionally detached. This causes them a lot of suffering and dissatisfaction. However, this suffering results from a desire to have attention, which replaces a healthy human desire for connection. This happens because of abuse or neglect.

They need comfort

Psychopaths experience grief like other people. In fact, the death of someone they consider to be close to them can induce the same amount of pain and sadness as to the ordinary person. Some might cry and have similar emotional responses to trauma as other people. However, to them, trauma is often suppressed.

Psychopaths can also be hypersensitive to specific emotions. This often goes for their sense of control, loneliness, hopelessness, and powerlessness. Psychopaths feel a certain sense of happiness when they are committing acts that go against the social norm. They are easily bored, so they strive for stimulation.

How Psychopaths Use 'Love' to Manipulate?

Psychopaths manipulate with love, which makes their impact on their family's well-being that much more severe. With no emotional capacity, many psychopaths are skillful in making people do what they want for the sake of love. Most people associate psychopathy with criminals and murderers. However, not all psychopaths are prone to criminal behavior. While antisocial behavior, arrogance, dishonesty, and the disregard for others are common traits of a psychopath, their exterior is often a stark contrast to their personality.

Emotional Machiavellians

Psychopaths manipulate using their emotional intelligence. Emotional intelligence embodies a person's ability to manage, understand, and identify emotions in themselves and others. In general, we think of people who are more emotionally intelligent as kind and good to others. The truth is, emotional intelligence also has a dark side in the person's ability to manipulate emotions.

A dark side to emotional intelligence manifests in a psychopath's ability to use the knowledge of others' emotions to manipulate. Psychopaths can talk around their manipulation even when they are called out on it. They will find a way to alter or at least try to find a way to change the person's perception of the situation. In general, they use emotional intelligence for their own gain.

Research confirms that psychopaths can portray perfect empathy without significant inner response. They seem as empathetic as any other person. However, this response is only superficial. When analyzing the brains of psychopaths, researchers tried to see whether their minds will be activated by the sights of physical and emotional hurt. The results of this research suggest that psychopaths had a lower response in their brains to the suffering of others. This explains why they can commit crimes or harm other people without feeling guilty. Simultaneously, they can look charming. Regardless of circumstances, they can put on a smile and appear engaging if they feel like they have something to gain. The ability of emotional disguise enables psychopaths to fake love when they have zero actual feeling.

Psychopaths mainly use deception for manipulation. To manipulate with love, psychopaths use the following strategies:

Charm

Charm is one of the main character traits of psychopaths. They know how to act to gain an advantage. They operate in a smooth manner. Because of their low emotional responses, they often trick the lie detectors. They stay calm when pressured. In that state, they tell the most incredible stories that are straight-up lies.

Another way to catch the psychopath who is using their term against you is to notice if they deflect conversations. They will try to switch your focus from the topic of conversation to flattery. They will use affection to divert the conversation. With a loving face and a gentle touch, they will sway you from questioning their stories and their motives.

Flawed logic

Psychopaths often manipulate using false analogies. They use figurative ways of speech to persuade you into inaccurate, irrational ideas.

- For example, if a psychopath discovers your desire for a family and the insecurity in your ability to have one, they'll tell you that love can overcome any obstacles. This way, they'll sway you into forgetting about your insecurities and starting a family with them. Once your insecurities start getting the best of you, they'll use them in their favor. If you believe you're an incompetent parent, they'll lead you to think you shouldn't do anything without their approval. That includes handling money, child-rearing, and getting back to work. Opposite to that, a genuine person would acknowledge your insecurities and wait until you work through them to start a family. The first person wants you weak, and the other wants you strong.

Manipulators can spark a strong emotional response in you. For example, if a psychopath wants to get you to lend them money, they will use metaphors related to love that depict that the love is worth all the risk. You'll do something for them that goes against your beliefs, like getting a loan you can't pay off. They will use false analogies that make immoral and unwise actions justified.

Insult and slander

When pushed into a corner, psychopaths will use insults and slander. They will slander one's reputation to get out of a bad situation. Psychopaths also use slander to discredit opponents, including your family.

Emotional fog

A psychopath will find a way to make you feel guilty for their wrongdoings. When you're about to uncover a psychopath's lies, they will use every tool they have to sway you from doing so. For this, they will use circumlocution. They will beat around the bush, avoiding answering directly to a straightforward question. Usually, they'll try to change the subject or simply lie. If they notice that the lie isn't being effective, they will try to change the subject.

In a confrontation, they will resort to either criticism or flattery. This is all done to cloud your judgment.

Evasiveness

Psychopaths manipulate with evasiveness. They will answer vaguely to a direct question. This way, they avoid answering specific questions about themselves and their actions.

Deflecting guilt

Psychopath's first response to being called out for something that they've done will be to blame someone else. They will blame another person even if it entails lying. If not you, they will blame their family, friends, society, or the entirety of humanity. No matter what evidence you present them with, they won't act accountable.

Still, keep in mind that being manipulative doesn't make one a psychopath. Manipulation is a tool many people use to achieve what they want. The best way to describe how psychopaths manipulate with love is to say that they use your emotional vulnerability and attachment to them to deflect from real facts.

Lies

This leads us to the next behavior typical for psychopaths, which is lying. Lying is another one of the main traits of a psychopath. When beating around the bush or manipulating doesn't do the trick, that they will fabricate details. You can catch these lies because they tend to change their stories a lot. They will also fabricate the information so that your mind is now deflected from the question you asked. This is a method of improvisation to deflect your attention from them and their actions to something else using your emotions.

Being emotionally manipulated is perhaps the most toxic and harmful effect of being in a relationship with a psychopath. They will use your love for them to make you believe them over anyone else. They will do this by isolating you from other people in your life. This is also a strategy to deflect from revealing actual facts they are being asked about or accepting responsibility for their actions. When they have you wrapped around their finger in a codependent relationship, you will want to believe them over anyone else. If that doesn't work, the psychopath will also prey on your feelings of hopelessness and emotional attachment. If confronted with facts, they will play upon the fact that you will be unhappy without them, using emotional blackmail to get you to regret questioning them.

Emotional deception

Emotional deception is another way in which psychopaths use emotions to manipulate. They use one person to lie to another person. They do this by encouraging antagonism. If you hear stories about them from your friend or a family member, and you confront a psychopath with this information, they will use everything they know about your relationship with that other person to stay in control. For example, if your mother informs you that your partner is cheating on you, they will deflect the story from cheating to highlighting the problems you have in the relationship with your mother. They will tell you not to trust her because she's being judgmental and controlling. He will make you think that your parent is trying to get in the way of your happiness. They can make it look like other people are speaking against them because they want to hurt you.

Distorting the truth

Manipulation using the truth is one of the finest forms of manipulation. That is a tactic high-functioning psychopaths often use most often. They will use accurate information for immoral purposes. For example, they can speak about an event that actually happened, but their ulterior goal might be to distance you from your relationships or smear other's reputation in your mind. A psychopath might use something they know from the past of your parents or coworkers, and present it to you in a way for you to question the relationship. In this situation, you can't really accuse them of lying because factually, they are not, but you can accuse them of how they're trying to use the truth.

What to Expect from a Relationship with a Psychopath?

Namely, psychopaths use relationships to benefit themselves in either gratification or money. A psychopath isn't in a relationship with you; it's not so that you can have a happy life together, but instead, it is to dominate and run your life, be in control of your money, and get gain sexual gratification. Whatever their motive is, there is no love in it and it revolves solely around their gain.

All psychopaths use similar strategies in intimate relationships. It's hard to get out of their web because they're good at tearing down your self-esteem and making you believe you're hopeless without them. Sadly, it's hard to notice these traits at first, because Western culture approves of many characteristics that can be described as psychopathic. For example, an egocentric, self-fulfilling way of thinking, ambition without regard to others, and lowering the importance of emotion in business and relationships are only some of the reasons why you may have failed to notice that there is something wrong with your partner.

Stages of psychopathic seduction

If you're in a relationship with a psychopath, you can expect them to act caring at first and then become cold and distant. If you maintain eye contact for a longer time, you will notice that there is no real emotion behind their eyes. In relationships, psychopaths often express predatory behavior. They're also territorial, don't like their belongings touched, and want to dominate. They will act as if certain parts of your home are solely theirs, and you cannot access them. Here are the following stages typical for intimate relationships with psychopaths:

- seduction

- love bombing

- bonding, when they use all the strategies to make you believe like they are your best option

- trauma bonding

After the last stage, they entrap and eventually discard you.

Seduction

The first stage is the stage of seduction. In this stage, psychopaths read your personality and figure out what kind of partner you want them to be. Next, they shape themselves after that image. They'll transform into any type of personality, depending on whether you prefer a masculine or a more submissive partner, a mature partner or a more child-like partner. In this stage, they will also mimic your behavior so that you feel like they are similar to you. They will copy your body language and even your lifestyle. This way, they gain your trust. They will also mimic the way you dress, the way you speak, the way you smile, your body language, your thoughts and attitudes, and everything else.

They might act according to your aspirations and values. With this, they will use their charm, good manners, and confidence to lure you in. There's a natural attractiveness to confident people, and psychopaths are aware of it. Perhaps they will try to fascinate you with their courageousness, which is actually a display of their careless nature, as discussed earlier.

Love bombing

In this stage, they will try to impress you so that you focus solely on them. They will aim to become your personal hero. They will act in ways to make you idolize them and make the relationship the main focus of your life. They will always go the extra mile with gifts and become your Prince Charming. They will profess love and act protective and caring. It might happen that a person flirting with you professes love slightly too soon when they haven't known you enough. The next time someone confesses their love for you, you can question they know you enough to start feeling like that. In this stage, they will want to make you addicted to their attention. They will aim to make you feel like you need them desperately.

Bonding

In the following state, a psychopath will use bonding based on lies to make you feel like you have now intimately bonded. They will tell you stories of their childhood trauma and make up many dramatic stories that they allegedly haven't told anyone else. These will be false secrets.

If you ever tried to track or validate the information that they gave you, you discover that they are untrue. If you ask them directly, they will use all the tactics of deflection mentioned earlier. To fabricate a story, they will use your 'weaknesses.' For example, if you are particularly sensitive to child abuse, they might tell you that they were abused as a child. If you are sensitive to poverty, they will tell you that they used to be poor. If one of your loved ones is sick and that's bothering you, they will tell you that they survived the problematic illness and make you feel like you share a strong bond.

Another important aspect of this is that you will also be telling them your secrets. You will reveal most intimate fears, desires, and experiences, many of which you don't want anyone else to know. A psychopath will listen carefully and wait for the right time to start manipulating you with these experiences and use them against you.

Bonding is the stage in which the psychopath will start to have sex with you. With an emotional background, sex will only further deepen the bond. Psychopaths are often intense in intimacy, which can be either gratifying or start to get violent. In sex, they will either act on your desires or try to establish their own dominance, depending on your personal traits and the type of a psychopath. However, your intimate relationship is tailored around the goal of making you addicted to him. In this stage, you will be spending a lot of time together and they will fully integrate into your life. You will become addicted to spending time with him and having sex with him. You will start to feel like nothing else matters aside from your relationship.

Trauma bonding

The fourth stage of the relationship with a psychopath is the trauma bond. In this stage, they will slowly start to act like their abusive selves.

They may become indifferent, verbally abusive, or even violent. They'll use many strategies to make you emotionally upset. This trauma will only enforce your connection with the abuse and enforce the mind control. The more the psychopath traumatizes you, the more you'll feel hopeless, weak, and dependent on him.

After the love bombing, you will find it hard to believe that he is truly the person he is now showing himself to be. You will want to make up excuses, which will be that you are the one who caused the abuse. The intensity of the bond makes you believe that they are the love of your life and that you can't live without them. In this stage, the abuser starts tearing down your self-esteem and becomes even more dependent. You'll become their slave.

Psychopaths use trauma bonding to absorb intense feelings, which they enjoy. This puts the victim into a state of altered consciousness. You are almost spellbound and in a state of cognitive dissonance. Deep down, you can't believe that someone who used to be so loving is now acting violently. The only way for you to explain it to yourself is to think that something is wrong with you. This is the beginning of your enslavement. From this point on, the psychopath will become more and more abusive, and your self-esteem will be even lower. With your self-esteem diminished, you feel even more emotionally attached to that person.

They will use emotional manipulation to seduce you back into their web whenever they start to feel like they're losing control over you. They will do things to confuse you and make you feel like you're insane. If you used to be a happy, confident person, you can easily start to question your judgment and self-worth.

Entrapment

The next stage is the stage of entrapment in which the psychopath will try to completely isolate you and submit you to their dominance. They will try to establish complete control over your life. They will initiate marriage or get you pregnant so that it's more difficult for you to get a divorce. They will isolate you from other relationships using many manipulative and violent tactics. They will do their best to distance you from your friends, family, and even make you quit your job. Ultimately, when you are all used up and a psychopath has nothing else to gain from you, they will leave you. This can happen either because of sickness, age or poverty. They will abandon you once you become irreparably damaged by the abuse, and you're of no use to them.

The Dangers of Relationships with Psychopaths, Sociopaths, and Narcissists

Being in a relationship with a mentally unstable person can have devastating effects. Under the influence of psychopathic manipulation, your health can deteriorate, your work and relationships might suffer, and your life can be overall ruined. Here are the biggest dangers from being in a relationship with a psychopath:

- **Emotional and psychological abuse.** Psychopaths use numerous techniques to cloud their victims' judgment and ruin their self-esteem, such as:

    o Verbal and emotional manipulation

    o Insults

    o Passive-aggressiveness

Loving & Living Psychopath Free

- o Staging situations and conversations for the victim to question their reason and sanity

- o Avoiding to give answers to straightforward questions

These behaviors lead to mental confusion in a victim. Because the abuser acts in unpredictable and ambiguous ways, you are always tense and on edge, not knowing when you'll say or do something to upset the abuser. This can have severe effects on your health and even cause anxiety and depression.

- **Physical and sexual abuse.** Psychopaths are prone to physical and sexual abuse and violence. They will use violence to establish control and dominance over the victim. They are very skillful in disguising the abuse using manipulation so that the victim is often unaware of being abused. When confronted about their behavior, a psychopath will blame the victim for his actions.

- **Damage to your career and finances.** Psychopaths enjoy taking away the financial freedom from their victims. They'll either sabotage their partner's career, or abuse their funds. It's common for psychopaths to cause a great deal of financial damage, including overspending, getting their victims to take out a loan only to squander the money on their own fun and luxuries, and even taking the money for false investments.

- **Isolation.** Psychopaths tend to isolate their victims and get in the way of their friendly and familial relationships. In particular, a psychopath will sabotage any relationship of their victim's that goes against their interest.

The Worst-Case Scenario

Violent psychopaths can have a severe and life-threatening impact on their victims. Some of the most dangerous outcomes of a relationship with a psychopath include:

- **Injury and death.** Violent psychopaths are no strangers to putting their partner's life at risk. Depending on the degree of psychopathy, a victim can be attacked and killed in an outburst of rage, or as a reaction to abandoning the abuser. On the other hand, psychopaths also use systematic poisoning and other strategies to put their victim's life in danger. This will happen when a psychopath has used their victim to the point of losing interest.

- **Health problems.** Living in constant fear, trauma, and stress can diminish the health of the victim. Anxiety, panic attacks, cardiovascular diseases, and other health problems that result from chronic stress, are only some of the health problems a victim of abuse can face.

- **Depression and suicide.** Living with constant abuse can cause victims to fall into depression or even commit suicide. The nature of the psychopathic abuse is such to destroy the self-esteem of a victim and make them feel like leaving the abuser is not an option.

How to Protect Yourself?

To protect yourself from psychopathic abuse, it's important to stay focused on your own health and safety. Here's what you should do if you suspect being exposed to psychopathic abuse:

Be safe

Do everything you can to distance yourself from the abuser. Open up about your situation to friends and family, and ask for police protection. If you fear for your safety, report the abuser to the authorities and request a restraining order.

Avoid them at all costs

The chances are that a psychopathic abuser won't let go of you easily. You may fall into temptation to meet them and talk to them, but this could be dangerous. If you doubt you'll resist talking to the abuser, make sure you're never alone and that you have someone by your side to talk you out of it.

Prioritize yourself

The best way to protect yourself is to make yourself your own priority. Avoid making your relationships a priority in your life. Instead, to recover from the abuse, focus on healing. Make your doctor's appointments, therapy sessions, treatment, and recovery, the primary focus.

Be spiritual

Understand the person's character traits and don't try to change them. Giving up on trying to change a person has a deeper impact than you might think. The roots of your vulnerability lie in the refusal to believe that some people just can't change. This way of thinking has a lot to do with your state of mind, which will be further discussed throughout this book.

Chapter 3
Female Psychopaths

"I don't really like you, but I'm so good at acting as if I do that it's basically the same thing."

— *Lisa Scottoline, Every Fifteen Minutes*

While most psychopaths are male, it's possible for women to have this disorder too. Much like men, female psychopaths are born with a reduced ability to feel and empathize. A female psychopath can be as dangerous and toxic as her male counterpart. She might be your coworker, a neighbor, or even a family member. In this chapter, we'll review female psychopathy and delve further into the behavior of women with this disorder.

How to Spot a Female Psychopath?

Unlike men, psychopathic women often show through their masks. Initially, they might act as a helpless victim or a generous friend, neighbor, wife, or a loving mother. However, when provoked, she will reveal her true nature. There are times when she will act on like to her character, belittling and berating others when she feels like no one will notice.

Two-faced

If you encounter this woman, she's acting nicely with you because she's gaining something. However, if you see her get into a conflict with someone else, you will notice how aggressive and unstable she can be. The sudden mood swings can be easily noticed if you look carefully.

A fierce competitor

When a female psychopath feels threatened, she will direct aggression towards her rivals. This can be both at work and in relationships. If a female psychopath is jealous, she will target the woman who she feels is threatening her. This will go beyond common jealousy. She will get involved in this person's life and use threats and emotional blows to drive them away.

Stalking and bullying

Female psychopaths are prone to stalking, cyberbullying, and verbal aggression. They are also easily triggered into rage. You might notice a friendly-looking woman become- infuriated at little things, like getting a wrong drink from a waiter or having to wait in line for too long.

Warning Signs of Female Psychopaths

Identifying female psychopaths is a bit harder than identifying male psychopaths. This is because female psychopaths start a relationship by acting kind and submissive. They want a man to feel protective of them. They are also less prone to aggressive behaviors. While a female psychopath is not a risk for your safety, she's a risk for your mental health. She has the same lack of empathy as her male counterpart.

They make you feel guilty

Female psychopaths will prey less on your fear and more on your guilty conscience in order to manipulate. All psychopaths tend to go through life by using the path of least resistance and obstacles. However, men and women tend to do this in different ways. Male psychopaths understand that they can use their strength to dominate. Female psychopaths know that they can use their fragility to make people feel sorry and protective of them. While acting as a gentle lady, she will feel superior behind your back.

Overly pleasing

A female psychopath can destroy a person's life the same way a male psychopath can. Female psychopaths use love bombing to target their victims. They use declarations of permanent love, compliments, praise and sexual gratification to lure their victims. This can happen both online and in real life.

However, just because a woman is acting this way, it doesn't necessarily mean that she is a psychopath. Women with low self-esteem and extremely codependent tendencies can also act this way. A female psychopath gradually starts to establish control over the relationship and her partner's life. Initially, love bombing serves to convince her partner that she's fully there for him. Much like male psychopaths prey on women's innate fragility, the female ones prey on the protective nature typical for men, and their masculine vulnerability.

What is the 'Love Bombing' stage?

Female psychopaths, much like men, use love bombing to seduce their victims. They start their grooming intentionally and patiently. They appear trustworthy and generous, only to start using their victims in all senses of the word later on in the relationship. Love bombing serves to enforce an unrealistic image and beliefs about an ideal romance. It lures their victims into trusting these women and being loyal to them without much proof of their own involvement and loyalty. This forms an emotional dependence.

As female psychopaths start to show their real face, their partners find themselves in disbelief that the picture that they have created for themselves is false. A fabricated identity is too real in their mind to be seen as a farce. A female psychopath will go to great lengths to mimic her target's interests, goals, and values. Since women tend to be more visual in nature, she will carve herself after an ideal of a partner that her target wants and she will completely alter her way of talking, clothing, her hairstyle and even her way of walking, in order to emulate that image.

The reason why it's so hard to resist the love-bombing of a female psychopath is that she's good at preying on typical male insecurities. Men tend to strive to look dominant in women's eyes and for women to respect them. At the same time, many men are insecure about their masculinity, and it is easy to notice. This is why flattery is so successful.

Another way in which female psychopaths manipulate is that they declare love before any proof of love was shown. It could happen after only a couple of days before the couple had any time to bond or get to know each other. She will find ways to ensure her victim that they are the most important person in the entire world. Slowing down the pace of a relationship is the best way to defend yourself from a female psychopath.

When she realizes that her partner isn't easily manipulated, she will lose her interest. Maintaining your relationships, goals, interests, activities, and particularly boundaries will show the psychopath that you are not her ideal target. It's typical for female psychopaths to lose interest in men who can't be manipulated and who won't submit to her will.

Dr. Herman Kynaston

Differences between Male and Female Psychopaths

Both male and female psychopaths share similar character traits. However, they display these features differently. Here's how female psychopaths act differently compared to the male:

1. Submissive

While all psychopaths are highly narcissistic, female psychopaths are less domineering in their appearance. They are more likely to show their tendencies further on into a relationship.

2. Passive-aggressive

While they may feel like they are better than you, they will still praise you. They will pretend to like you, but gossip behind your back. Female psychopaths are also different in ways in which they display aggression. While male psychopaths show their aggression actively through aggressive and violent behaviors, female psychopaths are usually more prone to passive aggression.

3. Dramatic

Female psychopaths love drama. They enjoy picking fights over small things and then causing their partner to feel guilty and inadequate. While there are more male than female psychopaths (93% of psychopaths are male), there are also women who can be both psychopathic and criminal. Female psychopaths rely more on their looks, seduction, and sex to lure victims in and manipulate them. They will use sex to get what they want. One of the strategies they use is to deny sex when something is not according to their will. In addition, female psychopaths tend to suffer more from anxiety and emotional problems and are more promiscuous.

4. *Always a victim*

They are little likely to confront you directly. Instead, they tend to spread gossip or make up lies. They are also skillful in gaslighting so that you question your own behaviors and even your sanity. Female psychopaths are a lot more skilled in emotional manipulation. Unlike male psychopaths, they will wait until further into a relationship to start dominating. They might even act in a submissive way, but manipulate their partners or friends through the attitude of a victim. In a fight, a female psychopath is less likely to threaten to hurt you. Instead, she will threaten to hurt herself.

Female Psychopaths and Relationships: Who They Target and How It Ends?

After the initial love bombing, a female psychopath becomes unstable, both emotionally and mentally. She acts highly emotional. However, under the surface, she's completely detached from others and uncaring. While her words are emotional, her actions are completely cold and neglectful. For example, she might lure a man into having a child with her by talking about her love for children. But when she has children, she will become completely uninterested. Here's what you can expect from a relationship with a female psychopath:

1. Control

A female psychopath will want to be in control of all aspects of her partner's life. She'll watch where they're going, go through their belongings regularly, and demand that they report on all activities. She might do this in a seemingly benign way, by acting concerned, or saying she doesn't like being away from their spouse. Either way, the purpose of this behavior is making sure no one and nothing compromises her dominance over the partner. She's ensuring no one is talking against her and working against any relationship of her partner's that goes against her interest.

2. Money loss

Female psychopaths tend to be even more parasitic than males. She'll want complete control over the victim's money, and won't be a stranger to debt. She'll treat herself with luxuries regardless of the financial capacity and manipulate her victim into getting loans and selling their belongings to please her. She'll make up devious lies and schemes to obtain money. For example, she'll fake illnesses to get the money for expensive treatments, or fabricate business investments to borrow money, only to hide it away or squander it on travel and luxuries.

3. Drama and threats of suicide

A female psychopath will cause a lot of drama in the personal lives of those around her. Whether a partner of a friend, she'll act carelessly and irresponsibly and then blame others for the consequences of her actions. When confronted about her behavior, she will resort to playing a victim and even threaten suicide to deflect the victim.

A Short message from the Author:

Hey, are you enjoying the book? I'd love to hear your thoughts!

Many readers do not know how hard reviews are to come by, and how much they help an author.

I would be incredibly grateful if you could take just 60 seconds to write a brief review on Amazon, even if it's just a few sentences!

>> Click here to leave a quick review

https://www.amazon.com/review/create-review?asin=XXXXXXXXX

Thank you for taking the time to share your thoughts!

Your review will genuinely make a difference for me and help gain exposure for my work.

Chapter 4
A Psychopath 'in Love'

"Some werewolves are hairy on the inside."

— Stephen King, Danse Macabre

Most psychopaths target either one or multiple partners to satisfy their needs for companionship and connection. While a relationship with a psychopath is an unfortunate one by default, it's essential to know that they act on their own perception of love. As they dread loneliness and isolation, psychopaths resort to manipulation to secure that their partner will stay by their side. The following sections will further explain how psychopaths act in relationships, divorce, and confrontation, and what you can do to protect yourself when you're trying to end a relationship.

Psychopathic Romance: How They Operate

The misperception of psychopathy in society can easily result in missing the initial signs. You might think of a psychopath as someone who acts like a loner or stands out from the crowd. You'd think your date couldn't possibly be a psychopath because they're smart and confident. However, it is the exact opposite. Psychopaths can be well integrated into society. In addition, there's also a broad spectrum of this condition that makes it hard to pinpoint the exact symptoms. In other mental disorders, the underlying causes lead to symptoms, which then lead to maladjusted behaviors. In psychopathy, the actions are the symptoms of the disorder. Because of this, understanding the psychopath's motives is challenging. The most important thing to note is that in a relationship, a psychopath acts on their own distorted idea of love and companionship.

While their actions cause harm to their partner's health and self-esteem, they're driven by the desire to secure that the partner will never leave. It is a selfish desire, stripped of consideration for the other person. However, understanding the psychopath's motivation will help you understand the profound fear of loneliness that drove them to hurt you. There are a couple of typical behaviors that set psychopaths apart from most people when it comes to relationships. Knowing the psychopath's typical behavioral patterns will help you become resilient to their influence. Here are the most common traits of psychopaths in relationships:

1. *They move fast*

Psychopaths move fast through relationships, particularly in the early stages. They do this because they fear their partner will slip away. They will move quickly to sex, moving in together, getting married, and having children. Their spouses and partners will be unaware of the personality disorder because they are good at hiding their dark side. In the beginning, they can be fun and attractive.

2. *They're deceitful*

Psychopaths are prone to not only arrogance and dominance but also deception and gaslighting. Psychopaths reveal their dark side once they are sure that the target has bonded to them. This can happen after a couple of months or even years. Psychopaths are deceitful with the purpose of controlling the image of them you have in your mind. At the same time, they work to lower your self-esteem. They do this because they believe that the only way you'll stay by their side is if you have no one to turn to and nowhere else to go. Within the value system of a psychopath, they can be strong only if you're weak, and you'll stay by their side only when you're broken and hopeless.

3. *They're controlling and possessive*

Recognizing a psychopath is difficult, but predicting and understanding their actions is next to impossible. It's a lot better for you to focus on the way the person is making you feel instead of their own behavior. Recognizing a psychopath is that much more difficult because they put on a show of someone successful and confident. What's particularly interesting about psychopaths is that their thought process is slightly different than an average person's. It is a lot more hateful, angry, and filled with the desire to control and oppress.

4. *They're demanding*

It's impossible to make a psychopath happy. In a relationship, they'll be overly critical and demanding to keep you on edge. They want your focus entirely on them, and they'll make sure to occupy your attention with constant remarks. In high-functioning or borderline psychopathic personalities, these dark desires can be unconscious. They might actually think that they are helping you by controlling your life. They may think of you as their project and give up on you once you prove too weak to measure up to their standards. This way of thinking is common in psychopathic parents, and also in high-functioning psychopaths who feel like a partner is their trophy to show off.

As such, they might push you beyond your limits, only to abandon you if you can't handle their criticism.

Psychopaths and Divorce

Divorcing a psychopath is not easy, but can that be achieved with only a little damage. The experience itself is most often devastating, heartbreaking and frustrating because their actions are filled with slander, manipulation and low blows. They are also unpredictable. While an average person can understand why someone would not want to be with them, psychopath sees that as a great insult to their ego. To them, a divorce is a game in which they will want to win at all costs. The purpose of the divorce isn't to obtain assets or be correct in the face of justice, but instead to make you suffer and win the game.

How psychopaths act in divorce and in battle for custody

Psychopaths will fiercely battle for custody even though they are not really interested in children. The purpose of a custody battle isn't to get the children, but to hurt you by belittling you as a parent. Their passive-aggressive acts are tools to win the game and make you suffer. They will fight for every penny they can get. Particularly, they will fight for the things they know are meaningful to you. For example, if you want to stay in your home and you are willing to pay them off, they will not accept it. They will not accept any negotiations because their goal is to hurt you.

How to survive a divorce from a psychopath

Psychopaths are unable to understand the reasoning of someone who can make emotional contact for two reasons:

- They agree with anti-social rules because they see the world as an enemy.

- They filter the information in their mind to measure winning versus losing or being powerful versus being weak.

Because of this, reaching an agreement in divorce is going to be extremely difficult. However, there are a number of things you can do to preserve your health throughout the divorce and avoid further abuse from a psychopath:

1. **Cut all ties**

   The first tip to divorcing the psychopath is to prevent any engagement. Avoid feeding into their drama and instead allow things to unravel on their own. Now, more than ever, you benefit from acting like your abuser tried to train you: being a passive observer. Like a toddler having a tantrum, your future ex will rage and splash money on legal procedures, only to give up when they see they're not affecting you.

   Whenever a psychopath notices that something they say or do touches you, they will do it even more. If they are trying to contact you, simply avoid talking to them. Everything you hear from them is going to be lies, manipulation, or threats. If they try to persuade you that they will change, it's a lie. If they threaten, they might only do it to upset you, but make sure to stay safe. If they throw insults and low blows it's only to harm yourself-esteem. For this reason, abandon all contact.

2. Monitor and record

The next piece of advice is to document everything about your life and communication with the psychopath. Although it's less likely that a person without a history of violence will suddenly become violent, it's possible. If you can, record all of your digital activities and install surveillance in your home. Also, record all of your phone conversations, not just with the psychopath. This will serve as proof of your activities in case of slander and false accusations.

For example, if a psychopath accuses you of making threats, the evidence of your own activity can prove your alibi. Recording psychopath's threats, insults, verbal and other attacks is essential, but tracking your own activities ensures that the predator can't touch you without being recorded.

3. Resist slander and lawyer up

The psychopath will do their best to slander your reputation. You can sue them for that by providing evidence that their allegations are false and that they caused damage to your life and career. You can also use your own evidence to prove that your ex is a pathological liar, which will help in case of a custody battle. If you fear physical violence, or you're afraid that the psychopath might attack you, do everything you can to always have company. Also, make sure to install surveillance into your car, in front of your home, and inside your backyard. GPS devices and cameras are cheap and they can be useful in case the psychopath is following you. You can use this evidence to prove that they are stalking you.

4. Don't give them ammunition

Make sure that the psychopath loses interest in you. The less they know about your life, the less they're able to hurt you. Avoiding contact and not engaging can be successful with some psychopaths, but not all. Some psychopaths my feel irritated by being ignored.

Since you don't benefit from either irritating the psychopath or feeding into their drama, the best thing you can do is to try to make yourself look boring to them. Becoming boring in all aspects of life means to temporarily stop posting content on social media or talking to mutual friends. Instruct your friends and family to avoid talking to your ex. And if they have to, tell them not to share anything about your life that might be interesting to this person.

5. Avoid judging yourself negatively.

Understand that their behavior is solely their fault. You've been targeted because of your kind and perhaps impressionable nature. However, that doesn't mean that there is anything wrong with you and that your qualities are flaws. Appreciate your own good qualities and don't let yourself see them as a weakness.

Accept that emotional healing is going to take a lot of time. It could take years depending on the severity of the abuse, or whether or not there was physical or sexual abuse involved. You should be patient with your own healing. The emotional damage and the damage to your sense of self-worth is enough, let alone surviving violent abuse. Don't blame yourself for being unable to recover fast and don't push yourself into recovery.

6. **Stop trying to be right**

    The next tip is to let go of trying to prove your point. People who are outside your marriage may fall under the influence of your psychopathic ex. They may believe their story. Or they may think that you made a mistake for divorcing them. The same way you shouldn't engage with your ex, you shouldn't engage with others' views on your divorce either. If these people aren't significant to you, let them go from your life. Don't try to explain to people your side of the story if they are unreceptive of it. More importantly, let go of the desire for others to support you in your divorce.

7. **Look for a supportive environment**

    Oftentimes, it is the person who decides to divorce that receives the most judgment. You are facing the blame for not putting in enough work into preserving the marriage. Some environments go as far as justifying physical violence in relationships and advising people, women in particular, to endure through this abuse for the sake of marriage. In the eyes of many, nothing that happens in a marriage justifies a divorce. Accept that some people are simply narrow-minded, but they are not the ones who make decisions in your life. You are the only one who does that.

8. **Review and reflect**

    It's important to reflect on the experience so that you can fully understand what happened. Get clarification whenever you can. The more you learn about psychopaths and about ways to recover from them, the easier it will be for you to accept your reality. Get all the support you can and do the best you can to focus on your own personal recovery and growth instead of the other person. Practice mindfulness and self-healing to enforce your self-esteem and independence. Psychopaths and Confrontation

You've most likely encountered many psychopaths without knowing. The reason that you haven't suffered the same amount of damage from them as you did from your ex is that you didn't engage much. In confrontation, psychopaths are Machiavellian manipulators. Their goal is to win. You can't count on reasoning with a psychopath because they don't care. They care neither about the truth nor the effects of their actions. To a psychopath, your pain and anger are rewarding. Their ultimate goal is to see you suffer. Here's what you can expect in confrontation with a psychopath:

Unpredictable

A psychopath is unpredictable in conflict. Forget about obsessing and trying to predict what they will say or do, and instead focus on yourself and prevent them from causing more damage. If you are worried about their aggressive behavior, instead of accusing them of it, secure your home and yourself. In confrontation, a psychopath's only goal is to get what they want. They do this by using all of your weaknesses against you. They know what you need at the moment and they will use that against you.

Ambiguous

They will use conflicting messages to cloud your judgment. They will do their best to ruin your life by ruining your relationships and your work. If you are trying to get some distance from a psychopath, and they don't want to let you go, they will resort to all sorts of slander as a way of causing harm to your life.

How to Stay Safe

Either working or being in a relationship with a psychopath can be distressing and toxic. Psychopaths create a toxic environment by inducing stress in others and preying upon their character weaknesses. For example, if you have self-esteem issues, they might boost your self-esteem to gain your trust but then do their best to ruin it once you trust them.

While successful psychopaths tend to be callous, dishonest, and arrogant in nature, they can still put on a pleasant face. However, after this, they will be prone to exploiting others, placing the blame on anyone else but themselves, and imposing themselves on others. They will do their best to take credit for others' successes. Depending on the level of psychopathy, psychopaths can also rank higher or lower in level of consciousness. Successful psychopaths tend to act less irresponsible, negligent, and impulsive. However, that doesn't make them less dangerous. That simply means that they will spend more time planning directions and recording your weaknesses. Here are a couple of suggestions for you to stay safe when you can't avoid being around a psychopath:

1. *Focus on your emotions*

You can't affect a psychopath's thought process or their behavior, but you can focus on the way you feel. You can take away a psychopath's power over you by acknowledging that the way they make you feel is as an exaggerated expression of your insecurities.

2. *Be brave*

Losing your temper with a psychopath only feeds into their ego. Don't show fear. Psychopaths use fear as a source of control. They will make threats, stalk, slander, and do everything they can to intimidate you. Stay safe, but don't let them see that you are affected. It may not be the safest to say that they make empty threats. Regardless, don't show any fear, and don't let their stories affect you. If you are in the midst of a conflict with a psychopath, don't let anything they say get inside your head before you fact check it.

3. *Point out their flaws*

When you are forced to talk to a psychopath with whom you're in a conflict, gather factual evidence of their mistakes. If it's a divorce, collect factual proof of abuse, negligence, and responsibility. When confronted with this evidence that psychopaths will lose their power.

4. *Build up your mental power*

Work on your own mental strength, employing all of your resources and energy into making your headspace solely your own. Moreover, focus all of your efforts into nurturing independence. Codependency made you vulnerable to abuse, to begin with, and only by healing it will you be able to recover truly.

5. *Don't provoke them*

Aside from avoiding engagement, avoid getting in a verbal argument with a psychopath. Arguments with a psychopath don't have any chance of success and verbal provocation can easily spark a violent outburst. Only communicate with your ex through your lawyer. It is recommended to do that by delivering the information without asking questions.

6. *Monitor their actions*

Focus on their actions and not their words. If a psychopath is using painful words, threats, and accusations against you, take these seriously and report them, but with the same emotional cool they treated you with. If you're trying to determine whether or not a psychopath will act on their threats, look into their actions.

7. *Be diplomatic*

If you want to successfully reach an agreement with a psychopath, you will have to make a win-win agreement. You have to use arguments that make them feel like they are winning in the game.

8. *Avoid meeting them*

Avoid face-to-face communication with an abusive ex. Psychopaths are only successful in getting what they want through direct communication. Keeping your conversations digital ensures that you have the conversations on record, and strips the abuses of their manipulative powers.

Chapter 5
Conscious Defense:
How to Resist a Psychopath

"Some people stand and move as if they have no right to the space they occupy. They wonder why others often fail to treat them with respect--not realizing that they have signaled others that it is not necessary to treat them with respect."

— Nathaniel Branden, Six Pillars of Self-Esteem

Self-awareness is your greatest strength in breaking out of psychopathic manipulation. Manipulation is all about using insecurities to instill ideas into one's mind. Once you're aware of the ways in which a predator was targeting your weak spots, you will be able to set yourself free of their influence. In this chapter, you'll learn how to use conscious defense to drive the predator away and prevent them from harming you.

How to Protect Yourself against Psychopathic Influence

There are many ways for you to resist psychopathic manipulation. You often resist manipulation unknowingly when you think critically of media, friends, coworkers and everyone else. Psychopaths' manipulation is hard to resist because of their charm and flattery, and also because they shape themselves to both trigger you and cater to your deepest desires and insecurities.

Everyone has some history of trauma and emotional hurt, which leaves them vulnerable in many areas. Depending on how a predator relates to that trauma, you might be unable to see their ulterior motives.

Why is it so hard to resist manipulation?

Resisting manipulation is hard because it often gives a kind of emotional relief. It is disguised by our personal baggage, meaning that your emotional burden causes you to look away from the truth. The thought of being wrong is unpleasant, and you want to avoid it. You also might not want to acknowledge that you are being manipulated because of the sense of failure and shame that comes with it. Manipulation creates an imaginary reality in which your insecurities are healed. To set yourself free of manipulations, open up to considering the reasons why you might've unconsciously avoided the apparent truth.

1. Look at the bigger picture

Manipulation often relies on narrow-mindedness to cloud your judgment. It uses false logic, false metaphors, and analogies. So before you are convinced into something that seems outside your belief system, analyze it carefully. Manipulation often requires you to act without thinking through. Step back and think about whether the things you are thinking or doing are logical and justified.

Never question your rights or worth. Understand that your value as a person and your human rights are unconditional. Regardless of your history, no one has the right to take away your freedom of choice. No one has the right to do things to you that are uncomfortable. You don't need any reasoning to justify saying 'no' or setting boundaries. You always have the right to defend yourself in your rights.

Also, make sure to look at a person from a distance. Notice whether they act similarly with everyone or they paint a different personality for each of their social groups. Also, pay attention if a person is consistent in their behavior or they have sudden mood swings.

2. *Avoid taking things personally and blaming yourself*

Your toxic ex is the way they are because of themselves and you have no business trying to change them. Also, you are not responsible for others' behavior.

3. *Question everyone and everything*

Question everyone who comes your way and be open and vocal about things that interest you. In particular, when dating, insist on knowing their background. Initially, a psychopath will try to guide the conversation and dominate. If you start to ask your own questions and display mental independence, they will lose interest.

Manipulation doesn't always have to be a negative thing. Psychiatrists often manipulate psychopaths to act in better-adjusted ways. An excellent way to manipulate a psychopath is to show them how they can benefit without hurting you. They will have no interest in hurting you unless it benefits them in some way.

Negotiating with psychopaths so that they win something is also a good way to manipulate them in. Psychiatrists sometimes use bargaining to get them to act more socially adjusted. This means manipulating through exchange and giving fair value.

What Are the Psychopath's Weaknesses?

Psychopaths have only two choices in life: to either falsely adapt or to live in complete isolation. It might look like psychopaths don't have any weaknesses, but they do. Their biggest weaknesses lie in their feeling of detachment and the desire to fit in. Here are some of the major weaknesses you can use to drive a psychopath away:

1. *They dread loss and abandonment*

   They also suffer when they look at other people, their families, and friendships because they are aware that they will never experience that. Eventually, psychopaths can become depressed because of their lifestyle. As a result of this, their health often deteriorates. Violent psychopaths lack impulse control. They suffer a lot of loneliness and low self-esteem. These negative feelings often drive them to criminal behavior.

2. *They feel profoundly helpless and weak*

   Psychopaths also believe that the entire world is against them. The image of psychopaths in mainstream media doesn't help, as it only infuses the rage against the world. They feel isolated and detached from the world, which is an unpleasant sensation. Their violence increases as their anger and suffering increases. Many sadistic psychopaths create gruesome rituals to cope with this loneliness. However, the purpose of all this is to lessen the emotional suffering. Psychopaths deep down, feel helpless and weak and as a result, they hate weakness.

3. *They hide their weak spots*

They are devoted to hiding anything that makes them vulnerable. Fear of their own vulnerabilities makes them skillful in exploiting others' vulnerabilities. They think differently about what constitutes strength and weakness than other people. They also think of manipulation as strength and being hurt or abandoned as a weakness.

How to Be Immune to Psychopaths

Is there a way to become immune to psychopaths and sociopaths? Being involved with a psychopath causes a lot of damage to your self-esteem, like depression and damage to your relationships and finance. There are, however, ways for you to make yourself less likely to be a target to this type of an energy vampire. While there's nothing you can do to protect yourself from meeting a predator, there are always things that you can do to protect yourself from their influence:

1. *Give only to those who give back*

The first thing you should do is choose to only give to people who give back and who have proven themselves trustworthy. Psychopaths, sociopaths, and narcissists prey upon people who show a caring and nurturing nature. While you should nurture and appreciate this quality of yourself, you should also be careful about who you give to. Make sure to only give your attention and emotion to people who are worthy of it. Don't rush to be giving to someone who you just met. Instead, wait to

Loving & Living Psychopath Free

see that this person is open to emotion. Wait to see if they are willing to give back. This goes both for your assets, your feelings, and your efforts.

Giving to the wrong people can drain you physically, financially, and emotionally regardless of whether or not the person is a psychopath. When choosing people around you, including dates and friends, make sure that these people are as equally as giving as you are.

2. *Prioritize your own well-being*

Psychopaths use love bombing to isolate you into the relationship. The longer the relationship lasts, the more isolated you'll become from your friends, family, interests, hobbies, and even career. Prioritizing your own well-being over everything else will keep the predators away. Once they realize that you won't make them your own priority they will lose interest.

3. *Work to heal codependency*

Predators rely on personalities who seek others' validation to find a sense of purpose. Psychopaths use codependency to devalue you and to try to brainwash you into believing that you are unable to live without them. To overcome this, learn how to be more self-sufficient and independent.

4. *Prioritize your goals and financial growth*

Recovering from a psychopath is best done by prioritizing your own objectives, self-care, and safety. Prioritize your own goals and interests over a romantic relationship and over all other relationships. Never neglect yourself to please someone else, and focus on becoming financially independent. While some psychopaths aim to leech off their victims, others prefer to isolate them at home. Either way, commit to growing your financial independence and don't give it up for anyone.

Being financially independent enables you to leave a toxic relationship and setting your own boundaries with money drives the predators away. When a predator knows you won't join bank accounts too soon, or that you won't allow them to use your credit card, they will see that you can be manipulated and they will lose interest. Instead of investing in your relationships, invest in yourself.

5. Define boundaries

Do a lot of soul searching and discover where your boundaries lie. What is it that you won't put up with? What are the things you believe are worth tolerating, and what are the things that are absolute deal breakers? Make sure to be well aware of your boundaries and don't allow anyone to crush them. Psychopaths, narcissists and sociopaths will groom their targets to intrude your boundaries because they want to establish dominance. Once you hold your own and they realize you can be dominated, they will give up. Discovering personal boundaries is also done with mindfulness and evaluating your own beliefs and core values.

6. Nurture healthy self-image and self-esteem

Work on improving your self-esteem and self-image regardless of relationships. People who depend on relationships to feel good and fulfilled are more likely to be a target for predators.

7. *Rely on your support system*

Your friends, passions, and interests will fulfill your life better. Instead of romantic relationships, devote to searching for your true self outside relationships. Predators often target people who depend on romance to feel good. If you are fulfilled outside of a relationship, they will see that there is no point in trying to use you.

Learn How to Influence and Defeat Psychopaths

Is it possible to defeat psychopaths? This is a complicated question because it entails the ability to manipulate a skillful manipulator. You could be able to do it if you came from a place of unshakable mental stability, independence, and confidence. However, if your confidence has been damaged, it is best to save yourself time and effort by focusing on yourself instead of focusing on the predator. There are, however, ways to use their insecurities against them. Here are the strategies that you can use to drive away a psychopath using their own weaknesses:

1. *Map out your insecurities*

Your insecurities can be a source of manipulation. It can be your personal history, problems with relationships, personal insecurities, or your family history. Whatever you feel insecure about, someone else might use that against you. Reveal these insecurities and work through them. The goal is to eliminate the emotional response to a trigger. Once your insecurities are triggered, it narrows your perception and vision. You're unable to see the person's ulterior motives.

2. *Be unemotional*

When talking to a toxic person, try to take everything personal out of the conversation and out of your mind. If you feel offended or emotionally hurt, understand that you are being manipulated and that there is no reason for you to feel like that. Also, don't show signs of emotion. Speak in a flat and concise manner without revealing anything that it's not necessary. Aim to detach yourself from the conversation. Asking a psychopath a personal question will drive them away because they don't like to reveal anything about themselves. Asking them how they feel about something will confuse them.

3. *Boost your emotional intelligence*

The best way to fight manipulation is to increase your own emotional intelligence. Strengthen your ability to look at whether or not someone is trying to manipulate you. This can help you defend from emotional hurt. You can create your own alarm system that will trigger when someone is trying to manipulate you or coerce you into actions that aren't in your interest or go against your beliefs.

- **Know your weak spots**

  Still, you shouldn't base your efforts on specifically defending yourself from psychopaths. Many people can act in harmful and toxic ways without being psychopathic. One of the best ways to sense manipulation is to identify when someone awakens strong feelings within you and can quickly put you out of balance. When this happens, think about what in their words or body language could have caused you to feel that way? What were the triggers inside you?

- **Know their weak spots**

  One of the best ways to defend yourself against a psychopath is to enforce your own self-awareness. Most people get manipulated by psychopaths because they believe in their lies and their words. The more you know about how psychopaths manipulate, the better you'll be able to recognize them and protect yourself.

4. Criticize and point out their flaws

Point out psychopath's flaws, especially those that benefit you and those that you can prove with material evidence. Being critical of psychopaths also tends to confuse them and drive them away. However, if you're questioning your safety, you shouldn't try this. Be firm with setting boundaries and saying 'no,' because, after a couple of times of trying to cross your boundaries, they will learn that there is no point to it.

Using these strategies, you will strike straight into the predator's weak spots: their ego and sensitivity to criticism. By knowing your own insecurities, you'll take away the main tool that a predator uses to get inside your mind. Simply by knowing what triggers your sense of inadequacy and what your deepest desires are, you'll be able to tell when someone is using them against you.

Acting unemotional, on the other hand, shows a predator that they don't have any effect on you. This will shake their confidence and make them question the utility of targeting you. Adding to that, pointing out their flaws proves to them that they're not the only one pulling the strings. A psychopath's ego is one of their greatest weaknesses, and they'll withdraw when it's compromised. While spending your time and energy on a psychopath isn't the best way to limit their influence, it can be useful if you can't avoid the person and you want to make sure that they'll stay away from you.

How to Divert Psychopath's Attention Away From Yourself

One of the best ways to remove a predator out of your life is for them to lose interest in you. Because most predators feed off attention, any efforts to battle or confront them will only enforce their confidence. Instead, you can make sure that the predator loses their interest by doing small things to repel them. Here's what you can do to divert a psychopath's attention away from yourself:

Show them the most boring self

As already mentioned, avoid making ways and giving them ammunition to use against you. Make sure to make your life look monotonous and repetitive. If you're moving on with a new love interest, make sure no one, particularly your ex, knows about it before the relationship is serious and stable. Don't report on your activities, including nights out, travel, time with your family, career success, and others. Make the psychopath think your life is in the same place they left it. This way, they'll find you less appealing.

Make them think they won

A psychopath will leave you alone when they feel like they have nothing else to gain. If they feel they got what they wanted, they will move to the next victim. Alongside your lawyer, work out a set of proposals to negotiate with the psychopath so that they think they won. Are they after money? Give them a home you secretly know is worthless and infested with pests. Are they trying to get custody? Work out a seeing schedule that gives them plenty of time with kids. If you suspect they're dangerous, make sure to voice and verify your concerns. If the psychopathic partner is still after your children, give them a bit of what they want.

Psychopaths generally don't do well with children. They don't care much about their emotional needs, nor do they have the skills to take care of them. Do the best you can to make a psychopath think they have won, and they will move on to another interest.

Take away the reward

Identify what the psychopath in your life is looking for and take that away from them. There are many things psychopaths like to use in a relationship, romantic or not. This includes the following:

1. **Money and assets**

   Do the best you can to make your ex think you're broke. There are a lot of ways to this, like moving your savings into a secret bank account, or staging damage to your assets that takes away their value. For example, if a psychopath wants your home, spread the word that it's been flooded, and make it look true using all means that don't go against the law. Your lawyer will probably know what you can do to make your assets look unappealing without breaking the law.

2. **Care and nurture**

   If a psychopath is after your caring nature, make them think you've changed. Make yourself look cold, distant, and unemotional. Stay cold to their threats as well as promises of change.

3. **Fear and submission**

   If your ex enjoyed scaring you into submission, and they've used threats of violence to keep you restrained, show them you're no longer afraid. Within the frames of safety and responsibility, act as if you don't care for their words or actions, regardless of how appalling they are.

Learn that psychopaths have weaknesses

Like all other people, psychopaths can bond to their families and pets and they can feel sadness for their loss. They can feel emotional pain. Sometimes, psychopaths can be sad for their inability to control the behavior or that hurt other people. They are also unable to create close bonds with people outside their primary families. They suffer because of that. Most psychopaths had little love and attention from their parents as children, which contributed to their condition. Psychopaths feel inferior to other people, leading them to tend to overcompensate with arrogance. They understand that they fit into their environment only on the surface and they suffer because they understand that they are unable to have the connections that other people have.

Chapter 6
Take Psychopath's
Power Away with Understanding

"I'm an 'intelligent' sociopath. I don't have problems with drugs, I don't commit crimes, I don't take pleasure in hurting people, and I don't typically have relationship problems..."

*— M. E. Thomas, Confessions of a
Sociopath: A Life Spent Hiding in Plain Sight*

Understanding psychopathy will give you an insight into all the painful ways in which the predator is living isolated and lonely. When you come to understand that they targeted you for their own desperation and not your 'flaws', you will take away their power over you. In this chapter, we'll delve a bit deeper into how you can set yourself free of a psychopath by understanding them.

Give Them the Benefit of the Doubt: Are They All the Same?

Only a small percentage of psychopaths become violent criminals. Most often, this happens due to additional damage to their minds caused by a traumatic and painful childhood. Understanding that not all psychopaths are the same will help you alleviate some of the fears and start to look at them from another perspective. The better you understand predatory personalities, the less power they have over you.

Not all of them are violent

Just because someone is a psychopath, that doesn't automatically make them violent. There are numerous types of psychopathy, and high-functioning ones tend to be well-balanced. The degree to which a psychopath is prone to violence depends on their ability to regulate anger, which they often use to cloak fears and insecurities. If you're dealing with a psychopath who is more self-aware, they won't act aggressively. Violence doesn't serve any purpose to them.

Not all of them are antisocial

In general, psychopaths don't care for society and the rules in the same way most of us do. They don't have an emotional relationship with the society, but that doesn't mean that they don't understand the utility of the rules. A psychopath may not appreciate the concept of fairness, justice, or equality, but they do understand the reasoning behind the rules. Rules and laws create a peaceful living environment for everyone, including them. The psychopaths who understand the reasoning behind the law are usually not against it.

Not all of them are toxic

Psychopaths who tend to act manipulative and toxic usually do so to defend themselves from their own trauma and feelings of helplessness and inadequacy. If a person came from a history of normal upbringing, and they are more self-aware than average, they won't feel the need to put down others to feel superior.

What is the main point of understanding psychopaths?

When you understand that not all psychopaths are the same, you'll understand that a predator is a type of a person who needs to feel superior to other people in order to compensate for their own trauma and insecurity. Your predator is a traumatized, troubled individual who needs to be in command of people to feel important. It is a trait specific to them, which sets them apart not only from most people, but also other psychopaths. By understanding their insecurities, it will be easier for you to break out of their influence.

Understand Their Emotional Disability

Removing the abuser from your headspace is essential to recover from psychopathic heartbreak and the damage they've caused you. You might feel hurt, and you feel like you want to get justice and closure. Ultimately, healing is a process you do with yourself. It is a self-led process.

Acknowledge their inability to care

The reason you won't be able to get closure, or any type of emotional satisfaction from a psychopath is that they don't care. For a person to say that they are sorry, it takes actually being sorry. While not all psychopaths are necessarily abusers, you can't really count on them to care about the damage that they've caused you. For this reason, taking the power away from a psychopath is something that is done within you.

Remove the predator from your head space

You can't take power away from a psychopath by confronting or arguing with them. Best case scenario, you can end up beating them down with arguments or scaring them away. But the damage that they've caused won't go away after they pack their bags. Their toxic influence is now inside your mind. Once you've broken up with a person and they've left your life, their influence had stopped. Now, the image in your mind of the other person is solely a reflection of your self-criticism.

If you're still haunted by the criticism and insults from the previous relationship, it is crucial for you to remove the predator from your mental space. How do you do that? The first thing is to stop trying to heal by trying to beat down the psychopath. This is impossible because of their low functioning limbic system. The genetic background of the illness doesn't allow them to change or feel remorse for the things that they've done. Essentially, you can't take them down because they don't care.

What you can do instead is to focus on self-healing. Learning about psychopathy will help you understand why the abusers actions resulted from their illness, and not your personal flaws.

Use their toxicity to learn about your value

Learning about your own value compared to the psychopathic disability will help you step out of feeling powerless and step into a headspace of empowerment. This will enable you to grow your own health, authority, power, money, and status. More importantly, you will start to regain spiritual peace. The reason that the psychopath still has a mental impact on you is because their actions and words are appealing to your insecurities, and understanding how severe disorder psychopathy is compared to your 'flaws' will show you that your 'flaws' are actually gifts.

Why psychopathy is a disability

One of the ways for you to heal from a psychopath is to understand their disorder. It will help you to understand their mind. By studying psychopathy you will understand why the person has treated you the way they have. To start off, you can understand that from the moment they were born their brain was different than that of ordinary people. An average person uses emotions to navigate their thoughts and regulate actions.

Thoughts come before emotions and emotions serve as a GPS for behaviors. Even in healthy people, all emotions are learned. You learned what is supposed to make you happy, sad, happy, fulfilled, or guilty. This results from a healthy cognitive process. A psychopath doesn't have that tool. Instead, their brain is capable of feeling certain negative emotions but hardly ever positive. For this reason, a psychopath doesn't get any gratification aside from fame, and praise. A psychopath doesn't get any emotional satisfaction from acting selflessly in any way.

Understanding this, you realize that the person did the things they did because they are unable to be happy. For a person to do good, they must be able to feel rewarded, and that reward comes in emotional fulfillment. Psychopaths are unable to be happy by making another person happy. The closest thing they come to happiness is the sense of gratification that they get through personal satisfaction. Moreover, psychopaths are deeply hurt and isolated by their inability to create connections. Even psychopathic killers are open to talk about feeling detached from the world, how that scares them and how lonely they feel.

How compassion for a psychopath helps you heal

While you may not be able to count on the psychopath to feel compassion for you, finding that place within you that has the strength to feel compassionate about them will help you heal. Understand that the person who hurt you suffers great emotional pain.

- They suffer because they are unable to connect.

- They suffer because they don't care about things that normal people care about.

- They feel isolated and detached and that scares them.

- The only thing that they are truly capable of feeling is personal gratification.

- They are angry at the world and feel like the world is against them because they can't fit in.

The world cares for a sensitive person, not for a person who lacks the ability and desire to connect. Knowing what a person who doesn't have the same morality as we do, can do to another person makes you probably value good people even more.

Acknowledge Psychopath's Spiritual Purpose

Psychopathy reminds us that altruistic morality is a choice. Deep down, most people are profoundly selfish in their mental structure. A person's mental structure evolves and grows around what's good for them. However, when you have emotions you have an unconscious knowledge that what benefits other people benefits you as well.

The only reason because another person is unable to just approach you, steal from you, or attack you is because it's illegal. It is because humanity has reached the consensus that there are certain limits to our behavior that we want to self-impose to live in a safe and compassionate environment.

Next, psychopathy reminds us of the importance of selflessness. Selflessness is also a choice. People are in no way obliged to be selfless. No one can force them to do it. Still, the reason why, if you go to surgery or end up in a hospital, you can receive a blood transfusion, which can save your life, is because there are so many people who are willing to give their blood. The reason why people with failing organs are able to get an organ transplant is because there are selfless people out there who are willing to donate organs.

Psychopathy reminds us of the importance of altruism and selflessness. Now, with the damage that the psychopathy has caused in your life, you are more aware of how important and how wonderful it is to be altruistic. You will appreciate kind and good people even more. This insight helps you get into a head space of gratitude. Knowing just how many good people are out there compared to the predators can serve as a base for you to start trusting again and begin to open up to love.

Chapter 7
Get over a Psychopath
and Find Closure

"You can recognize survivors of abuse by their courage. When silence is so very inviting, they step forward and share their truth so others know they aren't alone."

— Jeanne McElvaney, Healing Insights:
Effects of Abuse for Adults Abused as Children

Repair the Damage to Your Mind and Soul

Recovery from all forms of abuse should start with owning your own right to heal. If you're reading this book, you've recognized that the true blame lies with the abuser. The turning point of your healing is to acknowledge that healing is a self-led process. The best way to go about recovery is to devote equal attention to healing both your mind and soul. To recover mentally, it's best to work with a therapist who will help you get your mind back on the right track. This means acknowledging that, while the abuser is to blame for their share of hurt they've caused, your role is to step out of codependency and move towards a more independent way of thinking.

To become truly mentally strong and independent, it's important that you learn to stop seeking validation in others and establish your own standards for making decisions and evaluating both yourself and those around you. Here's how to navigate mental recovery from abuse:

1. *Give yourself time*

Accept that recovering from psychopathic abuse will take patience and time. Depending on the nature of abuse, profound damage may have been caused to your body and mind. Many effects of the abuse could have left you feeling lost and worthless. The most profound damage has been caused to your self image, self-esteem, identity, and self respect. If physical and sexual abuse was present, you could also suffer from Post Traumatic Stress Disorder (PTSD). The best way to recover from a relationship with a psychopath is to have a self-centered plan of recovery. This strategy will include both spiritual and physical healing.

2. *Heal codependency and own your identity*

If you've experienced physical or sexual abuse, therapy will help you regain self-respect, a sense of personal identity, and relieve the sense of shame and guilt that is often present after experiencing abuse. Psychopaths tend to make their victims feel guilty of abuse and often unaware of it. What you have to realize is that the person has used mind control to break all of your boundaries and defenses and make you completely submissive to them. This has caused the profound damage to your self-esteem. Your therapist will work around the trauma carefully with you to enforce mental stability.

3. *Build up self-esteem*

Regaining self-esteem starts with becoming aware of your unconditional value. A good therapist will help you build up self-esteem by looking into the reasons why it was low to begin with. Low self-esteem usually results from insecure attachment to your primary caregivers. There are multiple forms of attachment you could've had with your parents or caregivers, out of which only one ensures a healthy, adult mind. It is called 'secure attachment' and comes from a relationship with your caregivers that based on unconditional love and support. The other forms of attachment fall under the umbrella of 'insecure', and include many types of relationships that shaped your mind to seek validation of your worth in orders.

Once your therapist evaluates that it's safe for you to delve into these issues, as it entails digging into childhood trauma, they will guide you through understanding how having insecure attachment to your primary family caused low self-esteem. Throughout this book, hints have been made that the reasons why you became a target in the first place came from your insecurities.

While nothing justifies the manipulation and hurt that has been done to you, it is important to understand that the tendency to seek validation in others made you vulnerable to manipulators. By default, genuine and kind people look for those like them, and those with high self-esteem seek like-minded people. Your insecurities might have been the reasons why you looked past many genuine people and bonded with a predator. A predator offered the opportunity for you to unconsciously heal old wounds by trying to change the person that was similar to the parent or caregiver who hurt you when you were a child.

Your therapist will guide you through understanding how and why you got into this relationship, and where the desire to heal or change the other person came from. With this knowledge, you will be able to look into your own self-esteem issues and start rebuilding it.

Heal in the Aftermath by Finding Balance

The effects of long-term abuse include anxiety, a sense of panic, insecurity of your abilities, feeling lonely and unsafe, and often being overly self-critical. To recover your mind after abuse, focus on balancing it and regaining mental peace. To do this, engage in regular therapy sessions and make sure to record and track your thought process. Looking into the ways you think and feel about yourself will help you pinpoint the exact insecurities and self-defeating thoughts that are bothering you. Looking into these thoughts will help you realize that they're factually inaccurate, and that you think more positively of yourself with a bit more work.

How to balance your mind after abuse

Knowing what happens inside your mind when you're in distress can help you navigate your thought process and find emotional balance. Here are the basic steps to balancing your mind after abuse:

1. **Process**

   The mental process behind healing from trauma revolves around learning how to process and validate your feelings, and learn your own value. Your therapist will help you measure the impact that the abuse had on your personality, including the way it made you feel both physically and mentally.

2. Evaluate the damage

You should look into the ways that the abuse made you think about yourself:

- How did it change your self image?

- How did it impact your self-esteem?

Becoming open to acknowledging the severity of the abuse and the impact it had on you will give you a basis to start rebuilding yourself and your life. Alongside your therapist, you will find ways to cope with the painful effects of trauma. These effects often include constant recollection of the traumatic events, the sense of guilt and remorse, and the diminished self respect. A therapist will help you acknowledge and cope with anger and sadness.

3. Don't suppress

Being open to processing all feelings that result from trauma is important to avoid suppressing. Suppressing trauma can cause numerous mental and physical illnesses and even drive you into drug addiction, eating disorders, or depression.

4. Plan strategically

Your therapist will also help you plan your life. Initially, they will help you establish a daily routine that will help you feel safe and secure. Alongside your therapist, you will review all aspects of your life from work to home and focus on planning as a way of shifting your attention from the traumatic experience to the present moment. You will gradually work with your therapist

Loving & Living Psychopath Free

to track the course of your thoughts and steer your recovery in the right direction.

5. **Open up to support and cut off negative people**

   You can rely on your support system to help you cope. It's desirable for you to open up to your family about your experiences and to anyone who is willing to understand and acknowledge your trauma. However, this isn't simple for everyone. The abuse could have been hidden from the public eye and your close friends may not be able to understand the severity of your trauma. Particularly in the case of marriage and divorce, people are prone to prioritizing the marriage itself over a person's happiness, safety, and self-esteem.

   The idea of preserving marriage is very much alive even in modern cultures. If you live in an environment where physical and sexual abuse isn't thought of as sufficient reason for ending a marriage, think about cutting the relationships off and changing your environment. The truth is that living in an environment where your efforts to heal and recover are being constantly beaten down will have a harmful effect. You shouldn't have to listen to opinions that you should have worked harder to save your marriage, because this can have a detrimental impact on your well-being. If you're in an unsupportive environment, do your best to move away and cut all ties.

   If your family is supportive, you should fully rely on them. Open up about the way the trauma has made you feel and rely on their love and support. Rely on your co-workers and try to be as open as possible about your history to get support. Do your best to rebuild your life and surround yourself with things that make you happy.

Establish Strategic No-Contact

Avoiding all contact with an abusive ex will help you get them out of your mental space. If it's not possible for you to stop talking to them completely, do the best you can do avoid direct, face-to-face contact. Whenever possible, keep your conversations distant and electronic. Communicating with your ex via SMS and email will limit their ability to influence you. Psychopaths are usually not very skilled in manipulating outside the face-to-face context. Keeping conversations in the written format ensures that they're all on record, and that your ex won't resort to manipulation, threats, or insults.

If you can't avoid seeing your ex because you live in the same neighborhood, work in the same company, or visit the same places, alter your daily routines to meet them as little as possible. For example, start shopping in different stores, and go to different restaurants and coffee shops than you used to. If you can't avoid seeing your ex at work, consider switching jobs, or at least alter your routines to see them less. For example, you can take a different route to work, or get there early to be safe in your office before they show up.

If you're still communicating with your ex because of children, keep the conversations short, on-point, and unemotional. Avoid getting personal and reflecting on the relationship, and focus solely on exchanging the details relevant to your children.

Create Lists and Compassionate Reminders

Now that you're finally free of the abuser, you can devote to living your best life and fulfilling your dreams. Focusing on yourself and personal growth will help you overcome the toxic influence and take your life back. Here are a couple of suggestions to do this:

1. *List your dreams and plans*

   - Create a vision board.

   - Set long-term goals for all areas of life, and break them down into steps you'll take.

   - List all dreams and aspirations, and commit to fulfilling them to the greatest extent.

2. *Affirm your recovery*

   Acknowledging your recovery with affirmations will help you establish a more positive way of thinking. It will also help you get through on rough days, when difficult memories start flooding back. Affirmations are a great way to reprogram your mind in a more positive, self-loving direction. When using affirmations, focus on the following:

   - Validating gradual and steady recovery

   - Validating self-worth

   - Understanding that the abuse wasn't your fault

   - Understanding that your abuser acted the way they did out of their own disability

- Validating your independence in thinking, living, and making decisions

3. Move on

Think of all the ways you can leave the past behind you. Freshen up your life to start over and move on using the following ideas:

- Change your look, hairstyle, and wardrobe.

- Change your home. Think about renovation or moving away.

- Change your routines and habits. Introduce something fresh and new into your daily routine, like meditation, yoga, or reading.

- Change your daily routines, including places you visit and the activities you do. This includes shopping places, coffee shops, gyms, and so on.

- Evaluate relationships. End all relationships that are toxic or otherwise unsupportive. Focus on those who are understanding and supportive of your change and recovery.

Use Self-Loving Mantras

1. **Debunk the critic.** The abuser could've made you think that your most valuable traits are weaknesses to be ashamed of. Create or find mantras to quote that revolve around an appreciation of love, sensitivity, and a caring nature.

Loving & Living Psychopath Free

2. **List the things you love about yourself.** Commit to list at least 10 things you like, love, and appreciate about yourself each day. Phrase the list as affirmations, and go back to it whenever you feel down.

3. **Validate love for yourself and life.** Express love and appreciation for yourself in a very straight-forward way. Acknowledge your right to say 'no', stop apologizing, and get used to standing up for yourself. One of the ways to exercise this is called 'The devil's advocate'. When you feel triggered or overwhelmed by criticism, act as your own advocate and lay out the facts that prove that you're worthy of love. You can do this exercise by yourself, or use it whenever you face unsolicited advice, ambiguous comments, or exaggerated criticism.

   Make sure to remind yourself of the love you have for your own life, and all of the reasons why it's worth living.

4. **Find positive role models and inspiration.** Many successful people, both male and female, started their journey from a place of trauma and abuse. Study successful role models and choose those who you identify with. Devote to learning from their experience and use their advice to heal and flourish.

The end… almost!

Reviews are not easy to come by.

As an independent author with a tiny marketing budget, I rely on readers, like you, to leave a short review on Amazon.

Even if it's just a sentence or two!

So if you enjoyed the book, please…

>> Click here to leave a brief review on Amazon.

https://www.amazon.com/review/create-review?asin=XXXXXXXXX

I am very appreciative for your review as it truly makes a difference.

Thank you from the bottom of my heart for purchasing this book and reading it to the end.

Conclusion

In this book, you learned how and why you became a target of the abuser. You learned that the mental structure of a psychopath, a sociopath, or a narcissist, is such that they are unable to love. You also learned that they targeted a person like you because they were looking for someone to use and control.

In this book, we've reviewed the features of the so-called Antisocial Personality Disorder, concluding that the people who are most likely to manipulate and abuse come from a traumatic background. You learned that there are inborn traits that make it impossible for a person to feel love and compassion. You also learned that early childhood that determines whether or not the person will be well-adjusted or not.

In this book, you learned how and why you were manipulated and what are the right ways to defend yourself. You learned that the predator's strength comes from your insecurities and need for validation, which they used to seduce and lure you in. More importantly, you learned the right ways to stop being influenced and become more mentally independent.

Perhaps the most important lesson from this book is that healing from the abuse is only possible once you get to know your own infinite, immeasurable, and unconditional value. Only by loving yourself, and opening yourself up to love, will you be able to heal mentally and spiritually.

Last, but not least, you learned that healing from trauma means healing from codependency. You learned that your attachment issues from early childhood caused you to seek others' validation and approval, which made you vulnerable for a predator. You also learned that the best way to recover from codependency is to become mentally independent. To do this, alongside your therapist, you will examine your own identity and value. The more you're aware of your real individuality, the more you'll love and appreciate yourself. Ultimately, the predator will lose their power over you as you remove them from your life and mental space.

DOWNLOAD YOUR FREE GIFT BELOW:

Go from Stress to Success with These 15 Powerful Tips

You're in The Tunnel, Now Turn on The Light:

Here are The Best Ways to Transform Your Success

Do You Feel Stressed-Out, Overwhelmed and Harassed Every Day?

Then you're stuck in a negative thought spiral that is keeping you from achieving *real success!*

How many times have you thought, 'if only I could be more productive, then I'd get ahead?' No matter how hard you try, it eludes you. Most people experience intense self-doubt, worry and negative thinking at some point in their careers. These are your immediate obstacles to success.

This guide tackles these issues with easy, direct solutions to help you break the cycle and get back on track. These 15 powerful tips will take you from overwhelmed to overjoyed, in no time!

This FREE Cheat Sheet contains:

- Essential tips on how to stop worrying and start living

- How to actually relieve anxiety and banish it for good

- Ways to get rid of negative thoughts, and how to stop them from recurring

- Tips to become the most productive, motivated version of yourself

- How to focus on career success and build positive cycles and habits

Scroll down and click the link **below to Claim your Free Cheat Sheet!**

I want you to know that you don't have to live this way. You don't have to feel like these negative cycles are getting the better of you. Your career is waiting to bloom – and flourish! Give yourself the opportunity to make the right choices, by learning how to authentically reach for lasting success.

Ditch the stress, embrace success.

Click Here!

Check out our Other *AMAZING* Titles:

Book 1: Anxiety and Panic Attacks
A Guide to Overcoming Severe Anxiety, Controlling Panic Attacks and Reclaiming Your Life Again

Relation of Physical and Mental health

Mind and body should not be thought of as separate from one another. They are both responsible for the proper functioning of a human being. If one health is declining, then there is definitely going to be an effect on the other.

People suffering from distress are 32% more likely to die from cancer than those who don't have self-induced distress about the disease. ("Physical health and mental health", 2019)[1]. Schizophrenia is also a mental disorder that doubles the risk of heart disease and increases the risk of respiratory disease by three times. Depression has been associated directly to heart problems.

This chapter would help in the realization that physical health should also be taken care of if you suffer from mental health issues.

Anxiety Disorders

There is not one identifiable cause of anxiety which will pinpoint its exact origin. However, there are some factors that are identified by researchers of mental health. According to them, these circumstances make us prone to anxiety disorders.

Anxiety disorders are more often than not appear to run in families. Although, there is no proof that genetic factors are involved. It may just be that environmental factors surrounding that particular household that are the cause.

Personality is the major factor in determining how we perceive everyday life and our behavior to our environment. More often, introverts are prone to anxiety than extroverts. Some people are perfectionists and some like to just get things done. Generally, low self-

---

[1] Physical health and mental health. (2019). Retrieved from
https://www.mentalhealth.org.uk/a-to-z/p/physical-health-and-mental-health

esteem arises from overthinking and poor coping mechanisms. All these things are mostly found in people who suffer from depression.

Neurotransmitters' lack or excess is also directly related to anxiety. Imbalance in them causes the anxiety-producing pathways to react more than normal.

Some illnesses such as long term heart disease or diabetes are sometimes the cause of an anxiety disorder. It might not be illness itself but a person's reaction to it. A feeling of helplessness can quickly bring on depression. If this is not identified and dealt with, then it will soon develop into anxiety.

Some hormonal gland problems have been directly linked to causing stress and anxiety.

Caffeine can make anxiety symptoms worse. Alcohols and drugs are also known to enhance the anxiety of the user.

Sometimes, a single event can turn it upside down for you. The occurrence of a horrible event may have had caused huge distress upon a person. Its consequences could be detrimental to a person's mental health. For example, abuse, the death of a loved one, a relationship cut-off, hectic jobs, etc. are some common events that have a huge impact on a person. It could also lead to developing severe anxiety.

Lifestyle Factors Affecting Both Types of Health

Here are some of the things you can do that would help in improving both your mental and physical health.

Diet

Ever heard the phrase "you are what you eat." It is true even though we eat every day, it's a common activity and we don't really pay attention to it, except those who are health freaks. It is a good thing to be concerned about what you are eating. Eating is one of the most important things needed for survival after all.

A good healthy diet will keep us healthy and the opposite will bring on a number of problems that make themselves appear over time. A healthy diet of fats, proteins, vitamins, minerals, and carbohydrates is essential to nutrition. The diet we intake can influence our physical health and it becomes pretty apparent to us over time. What we eat can directly influence mental health disorders such as Alzheimer's and depression.

Exercise

Any kind of positive physical activity is very important for our physical health. What we don't pay attention to is how it is necessary for our mental health as well. It is proven by research that doing exercise will release endorphins in the brain. They are feel-good chemicals that lift the mod. They will increase your awareness and energy. Even just walking for a while has an amazing impact on one's mood.

By physical activity, it means expending energy by movements that involve your muscles. Even just doing normal chores around the house will improve your mental health and you will have a clean house in the end. Exercise is a win-win situation for your body and brain.

Smoking

It is pretty much established that smoking is extremely harmful to your health. The funny thing is most people claim to do it for mental health reasons. They feel like they can effectively reduce their depression and stress through it. But it is only a short term solution and in the long run, its consequences outweigh whatever momentary benefits it presents.

People with depression are more likely to smoke than other people.

Cigarettes contain nicotine. It is a chemical that disrupts and alters chemicals in our brain. People with depression have lower levels of dopamine. Dopamine is responsible for inducing the positive feeling in our brains. Nicotine temporarily increases the production of dopamine. In the long run, it severely affects the natural ability to produce more dopamine in the future. So a person winds up addicted to smoking just because they think it is the answer to their troubles.

Effects of Anxiety on Physical Health

Anxiety has a considerable effect on our physical health not only for short term but also in the long run. If it, unfortunately, goes on for long, a person could develop chronic physical conditions.

When a person starts to get anxious or stressed, the brain sends signals to the body. Our body ends up releasing adrenaline and cortisol. Both of these are stress hormones. They are only good for the body when we are in actual danger, not for everyday life situations.

Some of the negative effects anxiety can have on our body systems involve:

1. Respiratory systems

Hyperventilation is when a person has difficulty breathing. It becomes shallow and rapid. This occurs during anxiety. During this whole process, the body intakes much more oxygen to supply to the brain. They often began gasping for breath as they feel a heightened need for it. Some of its accompanying symptoms are weakness, dizziness, lightheadedness, and the feeling that you are about to faint.

2. Cardiovascular system

As anxiety can change the breathing pattern so directly, it will also affect the heartbeat too. It can cause a change in heart rate and circulation.

This all is to cater for the fight-or-flight response your brain has told your body to do. Your muscles will start getting more oxygen and nutrients because it makes your body think you are in a fight with someone when really you will only be stressed for a test.

Hot flashes can also occur in the body. It happens when our blood vessels narrow, which is called vasoconstriction. Vasoconstriction affects the temperature of the body. After then, the body starts sweating apparently to cool down but then you end up feeling cold.

3. Immune system

All the boost our body gets from anxiety is short-lived and for the long run, it messes up our immune system badly.

People with more serious anxiety disorders tend to get more flu and colds.

4. Digestive system

Cortisol is a stress hormone. It is released during any situation where we are threatened or when under distress. Its function is to block off the processes of the body that are nonessential in a fight-or-flight situation. As digestion is not particularly needed in a threatening situation, it turns that down as well. Adrenaline is the culprit too as it blocks the blood flow and stomach muscles relax. As a result, you feel nausea and lose your appetite. It also causes diarrhea and you feel like your stomach is upset. There is also some research to suggest that depression can cause irritable bowel syndrome.

5. Urinary

So during a fight-or-flight response, it is natural to have an empty bladder. So that it would make us run faster. That is why we tend to get an increased urge to urinate whenever we are anxious or under stress.

Book 2: Living with Bipolar Disorder

A Survival Guide to the Misunderstood Illness, Bipolar Disorder, and How to Overcome Its Challenges

The treatment of a bipolar disorder includes medication, psychotherapy, cognitive behavior therapy, among other therapy options for maintaining a wellness routine. Experts have carefully studied medical treatment plans for a long time. Different kinds of drugs are used during different phases of the illness. Antipsychotic drugs are used in the treatment of mania. For a while, there has been a great deal of uncertainty and controversy surrounding the effectiveness of using antidepressant medications in the treatment of depression in patients. Lithium bicarbonate is a drug that has had the most efficiency in preventing relapse. There is uncertainty over the efficacy of using lamotrigine and other antipsychotic medications.

Even with treatment options readily available, many patients relapse with the illness within one year of diagnosis. The statistic is 37% of patients relapse into depression or mania and 60% relapse within two years of diagnosis.[2]

Treatment of Manic Episode

Jonathan was out of control one day. He could not be stopped. He went without sleep for one night. Couldn't sleep a wink, as he was feverishly working on a project for his job on the computer. The next day, he was delusional. He was talking ten miles per minute. He drank a gallon of coffee to make up for his sleep deprivation. After arriving at work, people began to notice that he was talking nonsense about work. He didn't usually behave this way. He was swaggering about how he was going to escape this job. He was immediately fired when he said that. His colleagues were afraid of what was happening. They said, "Jonathan needs help. We need to talk to him."

Many trials were done in the 1970s and 1980s on drugs such as lithium and chlorpromazine. And there were also tests that were done on antipsychotic medications. The results showed that antipsychotic medications were the most effective drugs to be used in the treatment of acute manic symptoms. This class of drugs includes olanzapine, risperidone, and haloperidol (Geddes and Miklowitz, 2013). Although these drugs were shown to be effective at treating the short-term effects of mania, the ones that demonstrated long-term efficacy in treating the symptoms of mania and preventing relapse included lithium bicarbonate.

---

[2] John R Geddes and David J Miklowitz (2013). "Treatment of bipolar disorder" *The Lancet. Volume 381*(9878), 1672-1682. Retrieved from https://www.ncbi.nlm.nih.gov/pmc/articles/PMC3876031/

Treating bipolar is a massive challenge for doctors and patients because much of it depends on the use and effectiveness of medical treatment. In addition to lithium, the antiepileptic drug, lamotrigine, has been shown to have a kind of placebo effect (Geddes and Miklowitz, 2013). Treatment of other antipsychotic medications has been shown to contribute to the benefit of many patients with bipolar disorder.

Long-term Treatment of the Illness

The most effective long-term medicine for bipolar disorder is lithium bicarbonate, which was first introduced by John Cade in 1949 (Geddes and Miklowitz, 2013). This medication has been used for more than 50 years, and there have been some studies that have been conducted to show its effectiveness.

At the same time, lithium is frequently not the only source of treatment for patients. In many cases, lithium must be combined with other drugs to have effectiveness as a treatment option. Lithium serves as a great mood stabilizer, but when managing other symptoms such as depression and anxiety, it proves to be rather ineffective.

While antipsychotic medications are used to manage the symptoms of the manic and depressive episodes in bipolar patients, they have less effective for long-term care, according to medical research.

Treatment for a Depressive Episode

Rebecca recently suffered from a bout of depression. Her mother died from cancer. She had spent three weeks in the hospital as her mother was receiving the final treatments for her brain tumor. Rebecca felt sad beyond words. She had no inkling of what to do with herself because she had lost a lot of energy. She could barely get up in the morning. All she only wanted to sleep in and not get out of bed. Rebecca knew something was wrong. She knew she was depressed and she wanted to get out of it. Soon, Rebecca knew that she would need to go and see her doctor, so she went to the psychiatrist to get adjustments with her medicine and to put her on some anti-depressants such as Zoloft. She felt herself getting better over time, but it took a while for her to recover completely from this depressive episode.

Rebecca sought the right kind of treatment when she was dealing with depression. She went immediately to her doctor and said that she was depressed. She didn't try to get on by herself. She sought the treatment that she needed through getting an adjustment in her medication. After she got this treatment, Rebecca was given a regimen of sleep medication (melatonin) to help regulate her circadian rhythm cycles, and she also had an exercise schedule. Because Rebecca likes to run, she was able to run laps every time she got depressed. She would feel instantly better if she knew how to deal with her emotions. By getting moving, she was able to deal with the problem of depression. Often, it merely takes taking a brisk walk, dancing to your favorite music on the radio, or even talk to someone, to get you out of the low mood and into something that is going to help you.

Rebecca realized that she needed to reach out to someone in need. So, she was advised by her doctor to talk to her friends and intervene in their lives but not feel guilty about it. Minor inconveniences are not a big deal in the long run. The best thing is to seek treatment when it is necessary.

In the case of Rebecca, she was able to get the help by talking to her friends and getting their counsel in the situation, which would greatly help her to recover from her phase of stagnancy and discouragement.

Rebecca got an appointment with her mentor. They chatted it up over coffee and talked about her recent depressive episode. The face-to-face interaction made a big difference for her. She felt loads better after their talk.

Face-to-face interaction is significant in recovering from bouts of depression. While messaging and texting are the ways of the 21st century, there is nothing that beats having a face-to-face conversation with someone. Rebecca was able to do this as she was dealing with her situation.

Rebecca then went to be a part of the Big Brother and Sister Club. She made an effort to help others who are struggling with different issues. So, she decided to mentor a little girl with ADHD issues. This made her feel a lot better knowing that she was able to help someone in need.

To provide for her ongoing treatment, Rebecca was able to help someone else. Studies have shown that helping others and supporting them is a way of helping you to recover from bouts of depression and gives you confidence, as well.[3]

So, let's look at some basics that can be extracted from this example of dealing with depression. What are some pieces of advice for dealing with a depressive episode?

1. Talk to someone about your feelings. Let it all out.

---

[3] "Coping with Depression." HelpGuide. Retrieved from
https://www.helpguide.org/articles/depression/coping-with-depression.htm/

2. Help someone else by giving your time to a cause that you believe in.

3. Meet someone face-to-face at a café or for lunch.

4. Ask someone to check in with you at different times during the depressive episode.

5. Take a long brisk walk or jog around the block. You will feel the immediate benefits of physical activity, which is proven to improve your moods almost instantly, given the chemical reactions of exercise.

6. Meet people regularly for some club activity that you enjoy. Having group therapy will enable you to cope more effectively with your emotions.

7. Talk to a pastor of a church, a teacher, or a coach about your problems.

Therapy as a Treatment for Bipolar Disorder

Another form of treatment for patients with bipolar disorder is psychotherapy. With psychotherapy, a patient speaks with a therapist, such as a psychologist to chart his or her moods and develop a treatment plan. Together with the therapist, the patient comes up with strategies to manage symptoms and stress and talk about how to maintain a positive and healthy lifestyle that includes exercise, sleep, and good habits to follow. The therapist is there to listen to you. When you need someone to vent to, you can talk to your therapist, who will listen, ask questions about your life, and provide you with the tools to manage your life with bipolar disorder. The therapist will be the person, who will be an ally with your psychiatrist in coming up with the right treatment plan. Your therapist will not be well-versed in the medication or scientific studies of chemical reactions. Instead, he will know things about psychosocial strategies, which will promote wellness in your life. Talking about your problems with him or her is going to give you the edge to be able to lead a good life that is free of anxiety. Your therapist will teach you how to identify your stressors and manage symptoms to prevent relapse from occurring.

Common Goals of Psychotherapy:

1. Provide early intervention when there are signs of relapse

2. Help the patient accept the diagnosis

3. Encourage the patient to continue to take the meds

4. Manage sleep patterns and promote good habits in all areas of life

5. Encourage the patient to avoid abuse of alcohol and other drugs

Book 3: Mind Hacking Secrets

Stop self-sabotage, End Procrastination and Develop unstoppable Confidence in 7 Days

Positive Mindset for Success

Many thoughts arise in our heads and disappear. If you get a particularly original one, the first step to bring it to the real world is by writing it down. Then, it goes from being nothing to being something. Writing is like a bridge between our mind and our reality.

The first step is clarifying your ambitious thought. Once you have an idea what you want to achieve, write it down and pen down the biggest obstacle next to it.

Keeping a daily record leads to a higher chance of success.

The main reason why some people are truly successful in life is because they have managed to turn thoughts into actions. In order to achieve our ambitions, the first part of the whole process is thinking about how to do it effectively. In the upcoming chapters, we will discuss the action plan.

Benefits of writing down:

You don't have to commit to memory because more often than not, we forget things. We are forgetful creatures. Some of us even forget our own birthdays. So, you can't expect to remember a random thought. It is better to distance yourself from it too so that you can focus on other things effectively without worrying about it slipping from your mind.

- You have a clearer and fresher perspective on the idea then when it was only in your brain.

- When you first have the idea, you aren't completely aware of its details and feasibility. As time goes on, you can see if it's worth it or not.

- You can write down some of your own thoughts after going through the recommendations of other self-made successful people.

- The worst enemy of creative and innovative people is their own mind, as it constantly instills fear in them. When you carry on with something you are passionate about, you will start seeing the effectiveness of your efforts. At first, it will be hard, but you will then see improvement in your ideas too.

- Ideas are interesting and it's a thought-provoking conversation tactic.

- Ideas motivate people. You might get mocked for suggesting something crazy, but there is no genius without a little bit of madness.

Virtues of writing down a schedule everyday

Sometimes, after a particularly busy day, you tend to contemplate. You have managed to get a lot done during the day but when you think about it, you realize you didn't achieve anything truly valuable.

It is very important to schedule your time properly, and when you do so, you will slowly start to see an improvement in all aspects of your life, including your family, friends, work, and yourself. After thinking and working, a powernap also helps you regain focus.

Scheduling is planning ahead and dividing your task by priority into an appropriate time period. By doing so, you will have a much greater chance of achieving your goals in time. If you strictly follow your schedule, you will see the following benefits:

1. Giving important tasks enough time to get done.

2. If something unexpected comes up, which often happens, you have a contingency plan to deal with it efficiently without disrupting anything in your life.

3. You get to know the limit of what you can get done without burning yourself out.

4. Sometimes, life gets so complicated that your personal goals get left behind. With scheduling, you will find time to work on them as well.

5. Many people are under stress due to an imbalance in their

work and family life. With scheduling, you can regain a balance between both parts of your life.

Time is invaluable, and it's difficult to comprehend just how important it is. The following are ways to schedule your time.

1. First of all, identify how much time you have got on your hands.

2. Find out which actions are expected from you in your daily life. Make sure you have enough time to perform them effectively all while following your timetable.

3. Identify and prioritize the most important tasks. Put those activities in time slots where you know you will be most productive.

4. Don't forget to leave out some time for the compensation of tasks. You need these, because sometimes, unexpected things that you can't ignore pop up.

5. In your schedule, don't forget to include some time to edit and review the schedule itself.

6. While reviewing your activities, properly analyze whether they truly deserve your time or not. Try to carry out those activities in the most efficient way possible.

Habits of successful people:

The following are habits of highly successful people that might help you in your journey as well.

Loving & Living Psychopath Free

- People who are at the top of the ladder all had one thing in common. They recognized the value of time. Here are some of their habits that you can easily incorporate in your life to achieve your goals with a positive mindset.

- They avoided making useless decisions throughout the day. For example, you spend extra time and energy to pick out an outfit in the morning. Most successful people stick to a dress code. You should try to automate the tasks that require your precious mental energy.

- People who start early in the morning are more productive during the day. They also have a more positive outlook on their day because they have more time on their hands.

- Try to introduce frequent breaks to your daily work routine. If you think that working constantly from the beginning of the day until the end is how you will get maximum work done, you're wrong. Studies have found that after 52 minutes of work, a 17 minutes break will maximize your workout. (2019)[4]

- Try to spend your breaks outside rather than indoors. It will boost your creativity and productivity much more.

- Multitasking causes more harm than good. Don't fall into this trap.

- If you have a bunch of tasks lined up, you risk getting burned out. Prioritize yourself and your health first, and learn to say no whenever appropriate.

---

[4] (2019). Retrieved from https://lifehacker.com/52-minute-work-17-minute-break-is-the-ideal-productivi-1616541102

- Don't panic whenever things don't seem to go your way.

Planning

Sketching out your plans:

In today's world, you may have noticed that small businesses don't really grow that well because they don't expand their presence on social platforms. They limit their businesses by believing that they have done enough, which is what leads to an unsuccessful business. For a successful business it is very important to sketch out every part of the business plan so that everything can be aligned in a proper way and positive results can be achieved. Similarly, we must outline our minds in accordance with want we want, in breakdown of individual steps.

Sketch out every part of the franchise, step by step.

We must outline what we want our minds to think about.

Note everything down, just like a well-written code. Strive for the most effective documentation, not the longest one or one full of explanations.

When setting up your goals, follow the SMART technique.

- S is for specific. Be clear and concise about your goals.

- M is for measurable. Your goals should be measurable, one way or another. For example, I want to earn this much amount. Give exact figures.

- A is for achievable. Make sure to set a realistic goal. Don't play around with the idea of goals. Take them seriously.

Loving & Living Psychopath Free

- R is for Relevant. Whatever you want should be relevant to your life. It should be based on your life. Don't try to become another person altogether.

- T stands for timeline. Don't be vague about when you want to achieve your goal.

The results we get are only going to be as good as the plan we employ to achieve them. Successful people stick to their action plan. They don't give up on their goals or dawdle on their plans.

Finding the path to your objective:

The following are some tips to help you on your journey to your objectives.

- All people have different habits and personalities. Some find it easy to stick to a schedule, and others don't. You have to sketch out your plans according to yourself. If something works for someone, it doesn't mean it will necessarily work for you. You must have a plan if you want to achieve something worthwhile in your life. So, make one that fits you best according to your weaknesses and strengths.

- Now that you developed a plan, take some time to work on it.

- If you are a highly imaginative and creative person, then your head is probably filled with all kinds of ideas. If you want to document your ideas and creative thoughts, it's a good idea to get a journal, which will also be useful to document your progress towards your ambition.

- Every once in a while, take a step back to observe and reflect on what is going on. It helps to keep you grounded and for you not to get lost in the crowd amongst people living without any real purpose.

- Act on your plan to achieve your goals. You will never achieve anything if you don't take action. Nothing worthwhile is ever going happen to you if you don't go out there and work hard to reach your goals.

- A complex problem is a wall. Break it down in steps to conquer it.

Don't be a Perfectionist

Don't try to be a perfectionist. If you are always stressing out about things being perfect, you will never complete your task on time, and worse even, might not even get started. You might have been so worried about it turning out wrong that you didn't even begin to work on it. It is impossible to be perfect in whatever you do. It's all subjective. Just worry about things getting done rather than them being perfect. If you are a perfectionist, you are certainly going to be a procrastinator. Don't get it perfect, get it done.

A lot of mental health issues can arise from always striving for perfection. Trying to be flawless all the time can put you under a lot of stress. People realize that they are not actually lazy, but just obsessed with perfection, and it's often too late for them to work on their goals or dreams. Nothing in life is ever going to be perfect; you just have to make do with what you got. A positive mindset allows you to be content with what you have rather than be sad at what is lacking in your life.

The following are methods you could employ to reduce the perfectionist tendency in yourself.

- Just try and get started as soon as you can. Try being a go-getter instead. You will make a lot of mistakes, but you will also gain invaluable experience that will help you grow as a person.

- Letting go of perfectionism doesn't mean lowering your standards. You can still have high standards. It just means you are giving yourself more room to make a mistake.

- You have to learn that you are not the one who has ultimate control over everything. All you can do is try your best. If you learn that, you will be much happier and at peace in your mind.

- Stop worrying and stressing about perfection with some relaxation techniques.

- The sooner you get rid of the perfectionist mindset from your life, the better. It is important to start with something even with less or no experience rather than waiting for the perfect time to start.

Complex Tasks

If you are suddenly faced with a massive, complex task, it is very easy to become overwhelmed and stressed. To tackle a big task, break it into manageable pieces.

Here are some ways to easily break down a complicated task:

- Make sure you understand the problem and its expected outcome. What is it supposed to look like after completion? Grasp the task fully.

- Try to separate parts of tasks. Make different steps and know which part should be done first, second, etc. Make an order that you are going to follow to complete the task.

- Set a deadline for each task. You will be more productive and focused if you give yourself a time period in which you will need to complete a task.

- Make sure that you stay on track. Remind yourself of the project in its entirety so that you don't lose focus.

- Always remember to set your timeline a little earlier than the actual final one.

- Work on the product thoroughly so that you can learn more about it and make it better with time.

- We always make plans for our life, but plans only work when you practically outline them to work out. You can't build a house by giving verbal instructions to constructors.

- It is best if you write down your goals. If you are able to vividly describe all your goals in written detail, you will have a higher chance of success. People who can distinctly describe their goals are 1.2 to 1.4 times more likely to achieve them than those who can't. ("Neuroscience Explains Why You Need to Write Down Your Goals If You Actually Want to Achieve Them", 2019)5.

---

[5] Neuroscience Explains Why You Need To Write Down Your Goals If You Actually

Loving & Living Psychopath Free

It seems like a tedious task, but it's definitely worth the trouble. Not many things make life more enjoyable than achieving your goals.

Writing is like creating something from nothing.

Writing things down has two levels:

1. External storage of an idea. You are not just storing it in your brain; you are physically saving it too. Put the paper you wrote it on in a place that you will see every day. Having a visual reminder every day helps you remember it much better.

2. Writing things down improves the encoding. Encoding is a process in which whatever we perceive goes to our brain's hippocampus. It is where the decision whether to store information in long-term memory or not happens. Writing improves this particular process.

3. When you write down goals, many cognitive processes are involved. First, you take a mental picture, then you transfer that thought from brain to paper. The generation effect is when people have a better memory of things they have produced themselves.

4. A study shows that people who take notes in the classroom remember more important facts.

Want To Achieve Them. (2019). Retrieved from https://www.forbes.com/sites/markmurphy/2018/04/15/neuroscience-explains-why-you-need-to-write-down-your-goals-if-you-actually-want-to-achieve-them/#3001926e7905

5. Daily reminders can help create positive loops in your brain. Overrun old habits with new ones. Mask the old tracks with new ones in your life. Bad habits can ruin your life in many ways, so if you don't recognize and get rid of them, you are going to be stuck in the same place your whole life.

Bibliography

Babiak, P., & Hare, R. D. (2006). Snakes in suits: When psychopaths go to work. New York, NY, US.

Branden, N. Six Pillars of Self-Esteem. Retrieved from https://www.goodreads.com/work/quotes/76620-the-six-pillars-of-self-esteem

Brown, S. L. (2009). *Women who love psychopaths: Inside the relationships of inevitable harm with psychopaths, sociopaths, and narcissists*. Mask Pub.

Epstein, M. A., & Bottoms, B. L. (2002). Explaining the forgetting and recovery of abuse and trauma memories: Possible mechanisms. *Child maltreatment, 7*(3), 210-225.

Hare, R. D. (1975). Psychopathy. *Research in psychophysiology*, 325-348.

Harris, T. The Silence of the Lambs. Retrieved from https://www.goodreads.com/work/quotes/22533-the-silence-of-the-lambs

Herman, J. L. (2015). *Trauma and recovery: The aftermath of violence--from domestic abuse to political terror*. Hachette UK. Retrieved From https://www.goodreads.com/work/quotes/530025-trauma-and-recovery

MacKenzie, J. (2015). *Psychopath free (expanded edition): Recovering from emotionally abusive relationships with narcissists, sociopaths, and other toxic people.* Penguin.

McElvaney, J. Healing Insights: Effects of Abuse for Adults Abused as Children. Retrieved from https://www.goodreads.com/work/quotes/24932844-healing-insights-effects-of-abuse-for-adults-abused-as-children

Scottoline, L. Every Fifteen Minutes. Retrieved from https://www.goodreads.com/work/quotes/41125525-every-fifteen-minutes

Thomas, E. Confessions of a Sociopath: A Life Spent Hiding in Plain Sight. Retrieved from https://www.goodreads.com/work/quotes/21583841-confessions-of-a-sociopath

King, S. (2010). *Danse macabre.* Retrieved from https://www.goodreads.com/work/quotes/1230142-danse-macabre

Printed in Great Britain
by Amazon